110660088

# ON BEING A POSTCOLONIAL CHRISTIAN

*Embracing an*
*Empowering*
*faith*

Diarmuid O'Murchu MSC

Copyright © 2014 Diarmuid O'Murchu MSC
All rights reserved.
ISBN: 1495957330
ISBN 13: 9781495957338
Library of Congress Control Number: 2014903429
CreateSpace Independent Publishing Platform
North Charleston, South Carolina

# TABLE OF CONTENTS

# ACKNOWLEDGEMENTS

Many friends and colleagues contributed – directly and indirectly – to the research and writing of this book. I am grateful to the staff of the British Library in London, UK, whose proficient and generous service made the research not merely more manageable, but quite a delight at times.

I owe a great debt of gratitude to Professor Stephen D. Moore for reading the manuscript, suggesting alternations and improvements and, more importantly, offering strong personal support. Dr. Marion Grau and Fr. Jose Maria Vigil also offered valuable insights to improve and enhance the text.

I am grateful to Gaines Hill of Createspace Publishing for invaluable advice and much encouragement in this my first endeavour with online publishing.

And as ever, my colleagues in the Missionaries of the Sacred Heart, and specifically my Provincial, Fr. Joe McGee, provide the resources and support so essential to every writer's achievements. Words are scarcely adequate to record my gratitude and appreciation.

# INTRODUCTION

Over the centuries, Christians have been indoctrinated into submissive loyal obedience: to God, to the Bible, but foremost to the Church itself. The patriarchal philosophy of divide-and-conquer has infiltrated the Christian tradition. To facilitate a deeper analysis, and a more informed understanding, Christians now adopt a range of social constructs to enhance a deeper quality of discernment. To the fore is the postcolonial critique, the subject of the present work.

The critical consciousness of our time – as illuminated through the postcolonial focus - detects in religion generally a psychological co-dependency (throwing one's life at the mercy of God), strong allegiance to patriarchal authority (emphasizing submission and passivity), and political posturing, using religion as a tool to dominate and control.

In Christianity, the dysfunctional collusion came to the fore in the fourth century when Christianity was adopted – and seriously compromised – as the official religion of the Roman Empire. The counter-cultural empowering vision of the Gospels – usually named as the *Kingdom of God* – was severely subverted, and kept well suppressed until scripture scholars sought its retrieval in the latter half of the 20th century. Even to this day, Church authorities are deeply divided on the understanding and re-appropriation of the Kingdom of God.

Meanwhile, modern humans are growing weary of such power games, and our tendency in the past to grant them religious validation. Instead, postcolonial insight encourages us to unravel the cloak of such control and dominance, challenge its monopoly, and evoke deeper more empowering understandings of faith. The reflections of this book aim at such a realization.

The envisaged audience for this book is that of *adult faith-seekers,* seeking a space that will welcome their questions, support their critical thinking, validate their hunches that things could be different, and provide insights that will encourage them to re-imagine their Christian faith in liberating and empowering ways.

# Chapter 1:
## *Colonial Christianity*

*All the texts that would eventually make up the biblical canons were produced in the margins of empire, but with the Christianization of Rome and the Romanization of Christianity the margins moved to the center.*
                                        Stephen D. Moore.

*Theology has been growing uncertain for centuries. Therein lies its greatest opportunity.*
                                        Catherine Keller.

Religion has been a long cherished endowment of the human community. It has been held in awe and respect, and those who criticized it were often dismissed as heretics or pagans. Religion has long been understood as God's gift to humanity, to be accepted in good faith, precisely because it comes from God. By accepting religion, and following it faithfully, we remain close to God, and hopefully will live eternally in God's realm when we complete our earthly sojourn.

There is no religion, however, that has come to us with an original divine purity. Every spiritual aspiration, whatever its source, is appropriated through a range of cultural mediations, symbolically, linguistically and structurally. We often end up with more human baggage than divine inspiration.

I support the view that there is a sublime meaning to religious aspiration, and a divine wisdom underpinning it. Religion and spirituality have certainly enhanced our human evolutionary story – although several theorists would disagree. Today, the negative impact is acutely felt mainly through religious violence in the public domain and a vast range of manipulative behaviors within the religious sphere itself.

In the present work, I dwell exclusively with the Christian faith, the one I have known best through my life experience. And I adopt one contemporary strategy – namely postcolonialism – to surface and confront what I consider to be the dark shadow of Christian faith in general, namely *the addictive lure of patriarchal power*. The power in question is much older than Christianity, and can be seen in the great Eastern religions of Hinduism and Buddhism as well (see O'Grady 2012). In Christian faith it seems to be rooted in the divine right of kings, with God and Jesus envisaged as powerful divine monarchs, an appropriation adopted by the Roman Emperor, Constantine, in the fourth century, one that has dominated the theology and practice of Christian faith ever since. Today, postcolonial scholars describe it as Roman imperial theology.

In this opening Chapter I want to trace the Christian origins of this dysfunctional development, and indicate its unfolding over the past 2000 years. This will help to illuminate the landscape that progressively railroaded the alternative vision of the historical Jesus, leaving us with an inherited Christian faith system, still enmeshed in a great deal of imperial dysfunctionality, and leading several contemporary Christians in pursuit of more authentic Christian sources that have long been subverted and undermined.

## Naming our Imperial Baggage

Having had no offspring of his own, Julius Caesar earmarked his great nephew, Gaius Octavius, to be his successor. Only after

Julius's murder on March 15ᵗʰ 44BCE, did Octavius discover that he was the new heir to the Roman throne, an honor he would attain only after he had ousted other contenders, notably Cleopatra Vll and Mark Anthony. He would come to be known as *Caesar Augustus* and reigned as Roman Emperor from 27BCE till 14CE.

The reign of Augustus initiated an era of relative peace known as the *Pax Romana* (*The Roman Peace*). Though there were still many foreign wars, the internal empire was free from major invasion, piracy, and social disorder. The 200 years of the Pax Romana saw many advances and accomplishments, particularly in engineering, road construction, and an extensive development of water aqueducts, all leading to commercial growth and economic prosperity. One of the most famous structures built during the Pax Romana, the Pantheon in Rome, has one of the largest free-standing domes in the world to this day.

The Pax Romana did not mean Rome was at peace with the peoples at its borders. Peace in Rome meant a strong professional army stationed mostly away from the heart of the empire, and instead, at roughly the 6000 miles of imperial frontier. The empire continued to grow and expand. By the end of his reign, the armies of Augustus had conquered northern Hispania (modern Spain and Portugal), the Alpine regions of Raetia and Noricum (modern Switzerland, Bavaria, Austria, Slovenia), Illyricum and Pannonia (modern Albania, Croatia, Hungary, and Serbia), and extended the borders of the Africa Province to the east and south.

Augustus, like his great uncle, Julius, enjoyed the exalted status of a divine figurehead. Frequently, described as the Son of God, and Savior of the world, he was seen as the continued embodiment of divine favour that so richly endowed his great uncle. His image was minted on several coins with words of divine attribution.[1] The assumption of the title "son of a god" by Augustus meshed with a larger campaign by him to exercise the power of his image. Official portraits of Augustus made towards the end of his life continued to depict him as a handsome youth, implying that miraculously, he never aged. Given that few people had ever seen the Emperor, these images sent a distinct message: his enduring youthfulness was evidence of his divine immortality!

Archaeologists and historians continue to surface ancient artifacts, witnessing to the extensive regard for Augustus as a divine Savior. In the village of Priene, in Turkey, at the entrance to a temple dedicated to the Goddess Athena, a large marble beam above the entrance reads: "To Athena, and to the World-Conqueror Caesar, the Son of God, the God Augustus." And an ancient Egyptian inscription reads: "Augustus: ruler of the oceans and continents, the divine father among men, who bears the same name as his heavenly father – Liberator, the marvelous star of the Greek world, shining with the brilliance of the great heavenly Savior."

The Roman Emperor was not merely a political figurehead, he was also *a divine governor,* through whom it was assumed that God's will for humanity and earth came to be declared and established. Many centuries later, this divine prerogative came to be known as *the divine right of kings.* But in fact it predated the rise of Christianity by well over 1,000 years. The title "Son of Heaven" seems to have been first used in the Western Zhou dynasty (c. 1000 BC). It is mentioned in the Shijing book of songs, and reflected the Zhou belief that as Son of Heaven (and as its delegate) the Emperor of China was responsible for the well being of the whole world by virtue of a heavenly mandate. Jimmu Tenno, the first Emperor of Japan (perhaps c. 600 BC), was also called the Son of Heaven.

Greek mythology also abounds with tributes to the divine status of outstanding heroes such as Heracles, Perseus, Jason, Theseus, Oedipus, and Odysseus, hero of *The Odyssey. From* around 360 BC onwards, Alexander the Great used the title, "Son of Ammon–Zeus," thereby adopting the status of a demigod. The reference in Psalm 2 to the king as the son of God implies the authority of the king and the confirmation of his being adopted as the son of God at coronation time.[2]

The Hebrew Scriptures clearly portray God as a ruling king, and the identification of God with kingly rule and power is very strong. God blessed the monarchy, and he even chose a kingly line from which to appear in human form. An impressive theology of kingship can be traced throughout the OT and into the NT – with a central focus on the great King David. The King is also portrayed as one who will lead Israel by being the covenant administrator. At the heart of this covenant was Israel's obligation to be totally loyal to Yahweh, as earthly subjects are faithful to kingly governance. The godly king was to lead the people in worship and in keeping covenant, and to trust in YHWH to fight Israel's battles.

We note in this description a dominant understanding of God as divine ruler, governing from on high, through a line of linear descent, and invoking violence, if necessary, to enforce divine decree which, in the culture of the time, also meant imperial rule. People are passive recipients, whose primary role is to obey and submit. Also worthy of note is the commodification of land – to be conquered and subdued, despite the Torah teaching that the land is God's great gift to the people.

## Jesus the King

The Hebrew Scriptures (OT) have long been regarded as the precursor to the New Testament, the latter being impossible to understand without being informed by the former. For Christians generally, the Old Testament evidences the honor and glory of God, evoking in the devotee holiness and faithful service. Most

Christians also base their faith on a strong dualistic split between the sacred and the secular – a distinction largely unknown when the Hebrew Scriptures were being compiled. The sacred belongs to God's omnipotence (all-powerful) and omniscience (all-knowing), and fidelity to such a God means gradual abandonment of all that distracts from the things of God in the secular realm.

On the surface, the New Testament faithfully reflects the divine imperialism, not merely in the Hebrew Scriptures, but as indicated above, congruent with a set of perceptions dating back at least 1,000 years. The genealogies in Matt.1:1-17 and Lk.3:23-38 make it abundantly clear that God's great deliverer was expected to arise from a royal line. In fact, it was more than an expectation: only one whose pedigree could be traced to royal descent would be accepted as genuinely messianic. Kingship and divinity were perceived to be synonymous.

And when Jesus announces God's new breakthrough in terms of the *Kingdom of God*, those hearing the proclamation in Greek (as distinct from Aramaic), would readily recognize the divine imperative. And those in the Gospels who seek to exalt Jesus to an imperial throne (mainly the male apostles), believe they are doing an act of God, showing love and respect for the ruling God from on high.

Things become even more complicated when we look at the various titles which the evangelists attribute to Jesus. It has long been assumed that these titles arose from some sacred inspired source. More fundamentalist scholarship tends to regard them as historically reliable appellations given by or to the historical Jesus. Such titles include: Son of God, Son of Man, Messiah (the Christ), Savior, Rabbi, Lord, King – adopted from the secular, imperial culture rather than from any revealed source. (More in Carter 2006).

All of which brings us to what Fernando Segovia (1998) calls *the postcolonial optic*. What are we actually looking at? And with

6

what eyes are we viewing the reality of our engagement? Where did the evangelists get the titles from? And who had the felt need to apply such titles to Jesus? What are the cultural influences as distinct from the inspiration that underpins sacred writ? We'll return to these urgent questions in Chapter Four.

Colonial influence in Christian history is often traced back to another Roman Emperor, Constantine (272-337), who in the fourth century paved the way for the acceptance and integration of Christianity as the official religion of the Roman Empire. This is certainly one of the more blatant compromises that has occurred in Christian history. Constantine unambiguously endorsed the divine right of kings, dignifying Jesus with a new royal title: *Pantocrator*, ruler of the whole universe. As illustrated by Rieger (2007, 70ff), much of the deliberation at the councils of Nicea and Chalcedon is influenced by this royal appropriation.

## Colonial Christianity in the Sixteenth Century

After Constantine, the identification of God's will for humanity with the wishes of imperial force became endemic to the development of Christian faith until the mid-twentieth century. Most Christian historians were born out of the culture of Christian imperialism. Consequently, the history of Christianity (often referred to as Church history) carries a slanted view, heavily tilted toward the enculturation and exaltation of patriarchal power. We see this vividly illustrated in the great Catholic Council of Trent in the 16th century (1545-1563).

For the Catholic Church, the Council of Trent is widely regarded as one of its single greatest achievements. In contrast to the invasive 'heresy' of the Protestant reformation, the council set out to clarify beyond all ambiguity the true teaching of the Christian faith. And this absolute truth was to be reinforced unequivocally by the divinely mandated authority of the Catholic

Church. Such authorization, and the unquestioned allegiance it demanded, was invested in one outstanding personality, adorned with imperial power: the *male, white, celibate cleric.* This closed ecclesiastical domain, with clericalism at its core, has yet to be subjected to a thorough postcolonial critique. Although a distinctly Catholic phenomenon, it was duly endorsed by all the other Christian denominations. When it comes to the appropriation of patriarchal power, the Churches are very much at one in solidarity and collusion.

I will comment briefly on each of the dominant features of the anthropology that prevailed in 16th century Europe and its Christian clerical evolution. Firstly, only *males* were considered authentic human beings, and to them alone would be entrusted sacred learning, and the accompanying responsibility for its development and dissemination. In this regard the Catholic Church was uncritically embracing Aristotle's anthropology, endorsed by St. Thomas Aquinas in the Middle Ages. Males alone were authentically and fully human; females were deemed to be misbegotten males[3].

Secondly, it had to be *white* males, that is, Europeans, as all other peoples were considered racially inferior. Only Europeans were deemed to be civilized, all others being primitive to one degree or another, and therefore incapable of assimilating the divine wisdom assumed to be underpinning the Council of Trent. In this regard, black people were the ultimate enigma, as blackness had a colloquial association with the power of Satan and the darkness of sin and perversion. The racist remnants of this prejudice continue till the present time.

Thirdly, we deal with the thorny subject of *clerical celibacy.* In the Tridentine context, celibacy has nothing to do with sexuality or human intimacy, as God was perceived to be non-sexual, and good priests were called upon to aspire to be like the angels, transcending all the urges of the flesh. In this way they would become more God-like, and thus could represent God in word and deed. In this context, therefore, celibacy denotes a quality of holiness equal to God himself. It is really an inverted form of power, a power which in due course would morph into several forms of abuse, which haunt contemporary Catholicism.

Finally, we come to *clericalism* itself, rarely named for its post-colonial indignation, and obfuscated amid a plethora of confused power games that take a terrible emotional and spiritual toll on priests and people alike. From my perspective as a social-scientist, viewing through a postcolonial lens, it appears that it was priesthood itself that proved to be the greatest casualty of the Council of Trent. By endowing the priest with such exalted, pseudo-divine status, the Council seriously betrayed the oldest definition of priesthood that had prevailed from early Christian times: *the servus servorum Dei* (the priest as servant of the servants of God). Authentic priesthood had long been understood as a radical form of service (an ideal it often failed to deliver). After Trent it became a perverse form of power, seriously subverting the vocation to service embedded deeply in Christian tradition. In the Catholic Church today, the confusion between *priesthood* and *clericalism* is at the root of many of Catholicism's dysfunctionalities. Not until that confusion is resolved can the Catholic Church hope to speak with integrity and truth to the contemporary world.

I seek to unravel the flawed anthropology of the Council of Trent because it helps to unearth dysfunctionalities that have roots much further back in Christian history, and it is these older imperial dynamics that postcolonialism is striving to uncover and address afresh. For instance our tendency to construe Jesus as a priest, albeit a High-Priest, belongs to a clerical, imperial mindset that has bedeviled Christianity from earliest times. *Jesus had nothing to do with priesthood in any shape or form.* Throughout the synoptic gospels, Jesus openly denounces the priestly system of his day, a stance that becomes more ambiguous in John's Gospel wherein Jesus tends to be portrayed in more exalted divine terms with echoes of clericalized status.

## Gender's Colonial Toll

Against the Tridentine background, we need to revisit the toll for women particularly. The divinely sanctioned philosophy of divide-and-conquer begins to take a heavy toll on the meaning of human life. In a thoroughly scholarly work, British anthropologist, Chris Knight (1991), describes the mutual interaction between males and females in hunter-gatherer cultures. The evolution of patriarchy, as the shadow side of the agricultural revolution, sidelined women and suppressed feminine wisdom. The emphasis on rationality in classical Greek times added further layers of oppression. For the Catholic Church in particular, it was the inflated exaltation of the male, while, celibate, cleric at the Council of Trent that crushed feminine wisdom to a level from which it would not recover for almost 400 years.

With the emergence of the dualistic framing of reality, and the background driving force of patriarchal domination, men came to be seen as real human beings, the powerful ones who could use reason and promote posterity in the power of the male seed, with the female sex portrayed as little more than a biological organism whose primary role was to beget offspring for the dominant male.

Males were useful, productive beings, females were considered to be a kind of raw material – like the earth itself - for the male to penetrate and mold into his own image. Hence, the recurring theme for much of Christian history, that female saintliness could be measured by the degree to which women could morph into being male-like. Although feminism in recent decades has tried to rectify this gender imbalance, and the misogyny that ensued, thus far, the analysis has largely failed, possibly because the critique is not sufficiently comprehensive. We have not mined the deep memory, nor have we healed the wounds that cut so deeply. Consequently, in both politics and religion, we find women adopting patriarchal roles, giving a semblance of breakthrough when in fact, they are colluding with, and further perpetuating, a value-system which we should be discarding entirely. This collusion is a useful example of colonial mimicry, a subject explored later in this book.

By the end of the fourth century, Christianity was well on its way to being another belief system of royal patronage, and its influence on the papacy reverberates to our own time. One of the last powerful vestiges happened in 1925 when Pope Pius XI instituted *the Feast of Christ the King*. In 1970 its observance was moved to the last Sunday of ordinary time and adopted by Anglicans, Lutherans, and other Protestant denominations. The feast was proposed as an antidote to the growing secularization of Europe, and peoples' waning allegiance to the Church and Christianity. But there is a more subtle sub-plot.

After the first word war, which ended in 1918, the political consciousness of Europe shifted significantly. People sought out more democratic, participative modes of governance, thus withdrawing support for the unilateral exercise of power adopted by kingly authority. Implicitly, Pope Pius X1 was appealing to the people of Europe to hold fast in their allegiance to kingly authority - since this was God's time-honored way of regulating human affairs – and not be lured by the free-for-all envisaged in the emerging democratic movements of the time. And let's not forget this move by the Church happens at the height of European colonization in Africa and elsewhere around the world. The divine right of kings had morphed into a universal imperial system determined to conquer for Christ the entire inhabited planet.

## What Kind of King was Jesus?

Already in the 19th century, Christian scholars – mainly Protestant – began to revisit the imperial culture embedded in the Gospel story. The notion of the *Kingdom of God* came in for fresh evaluation, driven in part by the first wave of the search for the historical Jesus (Albert Schweitzer 1910). Behind the imperial language the scholars detected a distinctive anti-imperial vision. It would be close on another 50 years – the wake of World War 2 – before a more concerted scholarly endeavor would seek to expose and counter the subtle and deep-seated grip of regal power on the Christian faith. What had gone largely unnoticed for almost 2,000 years now became the subject of intense scrutiny. And this time a transformative impact would ensue.

A growing consensus began to emerge around the central role of the Kingdom of God in the Christian gospels. While the scholars could not agree on a precise definition or description – and still can't – an expanding consensus emerged. If we want to access the mind of the historical Jesus, and strive to understand his liberating vision as initially intended, then we need to continue research and discernment on what the Kingdom means and how we embrace it in daily living.

Clearly, a fresh understanding of *the parables* is essential to this undertaking. Moving away from the tendency to allegorize the parables, or at times, over-spiritualize them, insights from the social and archaeological sciences helped to illuminate the original context in which the stories were told, with their often subversive and liberating intent. Thus the Kingdom of God came to be understood as Christianity's dangerous memory, purporting a radical freedom and emancipation from all that enslaves and corrupts the human spirit. And the focus was not merely on the personal and interpersonal; the social and systemic aspects of life were also subjected to a penetrating critique.

A growing gap began to open up – and still needs to be bridged – between the preachers and catechists on the one hand, and the scripture scholars on the other. Essentially, we were encountering two images of God and Jesus, a popular pastoral one modeled on dominating values of patriarchy, and an increasing scholarly orientation portraying the historical Jesus as a catalyst seeking the liberation and freedom of all. Clearly, the Kingdom of God belongs to the latter rather than to the former (as illustrated in Chapter Five).

In what sense was Jesus a king at all? Is he not the subject of many crude patriarchal projections? And how do we rescue Jesus from the colonial trap in which we have ensnared him? To such questions we also need to add: how do we liberate the Christian people from the indoctrination that has been so subtle and pervasive over many centuries?

These are the questions posed by the *postcolonialists*. How do we awaken people to the residue of colonial subjugation that prevails much more extensively than many of us realize. And how do we do that in a culture, and specifically in a Church, still structured and organized along distinctive patriarchal lines?

## Living the Questions

In 1994, Pope John Paul 2 evoked a range of reactions across the Catholic world when he made a strong demand (not merely a suggestion) that Catholics did not converse about the ordination of women. People were not even supposed to speak about the subject. It was not to be discussed nor were any ideas to be promulgated on how it might be the subject of more serious Christian discernment. The Pope declared it to be a closed question.

This stance is a form of colonization, one frequently addressed by contemporary exponents of this new field of study. By seeking to control language, one colonizes people into fear and subjugation. However, in the late 20th and early 21st centuries, the strategy simply does not work. In fact, it begets its opposite.

Living as we do in a world of mass information, more people ask questions (about everything under the sun), expect respectful and informed answers, and rapidly lose faith in those who refuse to take their questions seriously. Moreover, in this information-saturated culture, the human mind is more restless, more curious, and prepared to raise questions few would dream of asking a mere fifty years ago. The threshold of the human imagination is now stretched towards horizons of meaning inconceivable just a few decades ago.

We are often told that power is in the information. Those with the relevant knowledge, and deeper insight, are advantaged in several significant ways. Those clinging on to truths of a former time, and those claiming that certain truths are absolute – and never capable of being changed - lag behind and lose the confidence of the masses. Another Pope, Benedict XVI, was quick to condemn this postmodern culture with its rampant relativism. He failed to realize that such relativism is precisely what safeguards us against the idolatry characterizing the monopoly of power in former times.

For the contemporary Christian, this is very much virgin territory, a bewildering landscape of diverse and conflicting claims. The predicament is made worse by the fact that mainline educational systems have ill-prepared us for this disturbing transitional time. Yet, the rank-and-file are coping better than those in charge.

Postcolonialism, therefore, moves in the direction of a double resolution. It seeks to highlight the complex nature of how power evolves and becomes insinuated in dominant modes of behaviour, beyond the simplistic divide of winners and losers, victims and oppressors. It also unravels the messy nature of power mongering, highlighting shifting alliances, complicit collusions, even to the point of the oppressed profiting from their own oppression. Postcolonialism may be described as a strategy for raising consciousness, sharpening our awareness, and refining our capacity for critical engagement with life and culture.

The postcolonial optic is particularly scary for those who feel they have to protect orthodoxy against the postmodern onslaught of our times, namely those entrusted with the care of sacred institutions, those who still believe there is only one final rendition of the truth. Power is under threat, the power of ideas, of language, of institutional control. A new freedom is being released, scary and promising. I suspect it is the freedom the historical Jesus brought afresh into our world. After 2,000 years, is it not about time that we unbind the message and let it go free?

# Chapter 2:
## *What is Postcolonialism?*

*There is no power relation without the correlative constitution of a field of knowledge, nor any knowledge that does not presuppose and constitute at the same time power relations.*

Michel Foucault

*For people in the west, postcolonialism amounts to nothing less than a world turned upside-down. It looks at and experiences the world from below rather than from above. Its eyes, ears, and mouth are those of the Ethiopian woman farmer, not the diplomat or the CEO.*

Robert J.C. Young

Postcolonialism has been described as a way of conducting a critique of the totalising forms of Western historicism (Stephen Slemon). Western colonialism has a variegated history, which can be traced from early Roman times, in which present day Ethiopia was deemed to be "the ends of the earth," through the great discoveries of other lands, particularly the Spanish invasions of the Americas, and culminating in the European expeditions in Africa and Asia from the 18th till the 20th century. There is no shortage of historical monographs lauding the heroism of the conquerors, and a substantial suppression of attempts made to research and document the ensuing brutality of humans and the exploitation of the living earth itself.

Postcolonialism reviews the residual effects of colonialism on cultures, how the insidious oppression can endure for centuries after the colonizing forces have left. It seeks to unmask and expose the subtle and sinister employment of the colonial mind-set, mainly on two fronts:

1. How the powerful - consciously and subconsciously – cling on to the 'divine' right to conquer and control, whether in politics, economics, religion, mass media, law, health-care, education, and social policy.

2. How the powerless acquiesce to, and become complicit with, the totalizing impact of this heritage, inculcating an extensive culture of co-dependency (Mellody et al. 2003; Wilson-Schaef 1986) and internalized oppression (David 2013).

As a field of study, postcolonialism is described by the Korean feminist scholar, Seong Hee Kim (2010, 9) as a revolutionary practice which ". . .resists all forms of exploitation and oppression and seeks to change the way people think and behave, disturbing the order of the world. It questions all kinds of conventional knowledge, systems, power, their relationships, threatening the privileged, demanding the well-being of all human beings."

It is indeed another attack on power, but engaging a deeper and more penetrating analysis, getting right down to the subconscious driving forces, while also highlighting cultural and religious validations that cut deep into our historical past.

## The Colonial Residue

Postcolonial thinkers recognize that many of the assumptions which underlie the 'logic' of colonialism are still active forces today. Thus people's acceptance of, and allegiance to, inherited truths can often be a collusion with imperial values that have long outlived their usefulness and thus hinder people from progressing in more empowering ways. Under the impact of advertising and powerful propaganda, black people may seek to emulate the values and behaviors of white Westerners, but the subconscious influence may be due to a deeply ingrained collusive admiration left over from an earlier colonial epoch. Hence, the prophetic stance of Nelson Mandela, upon becoming President of the liberated South Africa in 1994, chose to wear a Madiba shirt of boldly patterned fabrics (made from traditional Xhosa cloth with braid) and not the inherited Western custom of a suit, shirt, and tie.

One of the most enduring features of postcolonialism is *internalized oppression*. Over several centuries women internalized the passivity imposed by patriarchal expectation. Aristotle's infamous allegation that females are effectively misbegotten males still impacts on the inferior status of women in several major religions, Christianity included. Oppressed peoples often seek excessive attention and recognition, because of internalized disregard left over from earlier slavery and oppression. At a more personal level, suppressed childhood abuse – sexual or otherwise – undermines authentic adult development, possibly for an entire lifetime. Internalized oppression pervades contemporary culture, and may be most subtle of all in those nations and cultures that consider themselves to be developed and advanced. In making these observations, one can stand accused of not supporting victims; in postcolonial terms, I am moving beyond the dualistic split between victim and oppressor, seeking a deeper and more transparent integration.

There is a cultural expectation that we should speak well of religion, and refrain from excessive criticism. This in itself is a strategy of internalized oppression. It becomes considerably more insidious in religions such as Roman Catholicism and Islam in which transgression is open to ridicule and at times will be severely punished. Much more subtle is the rhetoric that seeks to understand and even justify such subservience; instead of

19

forthrightly naming the oppression, the internalized oppression forces us to collude with what we deeply suspect is wrong and unacceptable. It takes quite a transformation of consciousness (a more self-aware stage of adult growth) to name publicly what is stirring deep in our hearts.

The colonial mindset – what Robert Young (2003) calls neo-colonialism - pervades modern culture through the several patriarchal constructs that still prevail. The values of domination mediated through governance from on high continue to be an unquestioned assumption throughout the contemporary world. That those at the top know what is best for everybody else also enjoys extensive hegemony. Patriarchal power dominates financial management, social construction and ethical values. "Might is right" continues to be a prevalent philosophy.

Consequences, both overt and covert, ensue from this powerful monopoly. Most people are condemned to a perpetual state of passivity and co-dependency. Poverty, deprivation, and lack of basic human rights affects millions in poorer parts of the world, often leaving people feeling hopeless and living on the threshold of despair. Frequently, things are not much better in developed nations, despite an abundance of material goods and usually more than adequate health-care, education, and social resources. The dysfunctionality for Westerners shows up in the way we elect public representatives. Even poorer countries take great pride in being able to vote at public elections, but between such polling opportunities, the voter has little or no say in the ensuing quality of governance, frequently characterized by broken promises and extensive betrayal of what was initially promised.

All modern political systems are postcolonial veneers deluding people into thinking they are being empowered, when in fact they are being indoctrinated into co-dependent collusions intended primarily to uphold patriarchal domination. And in several cases formal religion unashamedly supports such co-dependent collusive behaviors.[4]

## Christianity's Colonial Baggage

What the present book seeks to highlight is the Christian contradiction, in which Christian leaders support and endorse patriarchal domination as an authentic expression of Christian faith. Christian history is riddled with postcolonial collusions, some of which go back to the Gospels themselves – perhaps more accurately, to those who initially pieced together what we now deem to be the foundations of authentic Christian belief.

By clarifying the imperial dynamics at work in the time of the historical Jesus, and the colonial culture of the early Christian centuries, we are challenged to name the blocks that still hinder the empowering and liberating message of the Gospels. By unmasking and unlocking the congesting power games, and exposing their divine validation, we set free the human spirit – and the human intellect – to understand afresh the foundational inspiration of our faith, and the alternative options open to us to reincarnate its empowering hope for the world of our time.

There are several features in the Gospels that have for long have been taken for granted, assumed to be of God and therefore prescriptive for an authentic spiritual life and religious adherence. First and foremost is *the culture of kingship*, explained in greater detail in Chapter Five. At the time of Jesus, the *King* was understood to be God's primary representative on earth, and all divine revelation was mediated first and foremost through the king and his royal dispensation. Earthly allegiance to royal patronage provided the surest authentic way to remain faithful to the expectations of divine royalty.

Next, follows *the integrity of the Jewish religion*, perceived to be the one and only context for religious submission to divine royalty. Judaism prides itself on being the first of three major monotheistic religions. The one-ness of God denotes the absolute integrity of divine power vested in the one only true God. As a cultural phenomenon, Judaism like many other great religions, was quite diverse in its evolutionary unfolding (cf. Arnal 2005); there were *Judaisms* rather than a clear-cut monolithic system to which all Jewish people subscribed, but that is a historical dimension that many scholars will not support, and for much of the 2,000 years of Christendom, New Testament scholars portrayed Jesus as a loyal and faithful Jew – particularly in his allegiance to the regal, divine father in heaven.

And a third dimension is the invasive culture of classical Greece, with its claim to rationality and civilization that proved to be so persuasive that it lured many naïve people into subservience to, and collusion with, patriarchal domination. The rational took priority to the mystical, humans set themselves over against creation, dualistic splitting fragmented the web of life, and masculine values of domination and control led to the extensive suppression of feminine egalitarianism. The Jesus of the Christian gospel became an anthropocentric projection of male patriarchs, and Constantine in the 4th century fully supported the distortion. Not until the 20th century did Christians begin to re-examine their flawed inheritance; the task of reconstruction is still a work in progress with quite a long way to go to reclaim a more authentic version of the original Christian inspiration.

## A Recent History

As a field of study, postcolonialism first became popular in the 1950s, when the plight of 'third world countries' began to impact upon Western intellectuals. Africa was very much the focus of attention, pursued in both American and European universities. Colonialism was running aground, as a new desire for autonomy and independence emerged. In 1960 alone, seventeen African countries regained independence. In the 1970s, this interest lead to an integration of discussions about postcolonialism in various study courses at American universities. Initially, the research focused on de-colonization, the process of colonial forces moving out while the previously colonized group struggled to reclaim a more indigenous identity. In several cases, ties were still maintained with the previous colonizer, and frequently, the colonizer dictated the terms of reference. So, in a sense the foreign alien influence still continued.

In time, the colonized country became largely independent, but by this time cultural customs and norms of the colonizer had been heavily absorbed. Attempts at reclaiming an earlier indigenous culture were at best ambivalent, and sometimes resulted in internal strife and conflict. The colonizers were gone, but their values continued to dominate and control the indigenous culture. It is this residual effect of colonialism – a type of cultural baggage - that defines the subject matter of postcolonialism.

The residue, however, is not problematic merely for those who have at one time been colonized and oppressed. Those of us who did not experience such oppression, particularly Westerners, tend to exhibit attitudes and perceptions that reinforce colonial oppression. Robert Young (2003, 2) states the problem as follows:

> Colonial and imperial rule was legitimized by anthropological theories which increasingly portrayed the peoples of the colonized world as inferior, childlike, or feminine, incapable of looking after themselves (despite having done so perfectly well for millennia) and requiring the paternal rule of the West for their own best interests. A process that continues today under the flag-ship of modern globalization.

Postcolonialism does not refer merely to the time *after* colonial occupation, but rather to the cultural grip still retained by colonizing forces who have long since evacuated a particular region or country. How we appropriate and use knowledge is particularly significant: "Most of the writing that has dominated what the world calls knowledge has been produced by people living in Western countries in the past three or more centuries, and it is this kind of knowledge that is elaborated within and is sanctioned by the academy, the institutional knowledge corporation." (Robert Young 2003, 18).

We are dealing, therefore, with a double meaning. Firstly, we are naming a political, economic and social residue of a powerful elite (usually labeled as 'the West'), which has impacted, and continues to influence, the growth and development of non-Western cultures, resulting in unjust balances of resources and wealth in several parts of the contemporary world. The second level of meaning pertains to how we use knowledge as a tool for power and manipulation; most of the literature on postcolonialism focuses on this second topic.

Knowledge is power and becomes increasingly so in the world of mass information which we now inhabit. Those who control the knowledge exert enormous influence on thought and perception. These include multi-media technology, advertising, literature, and centers of learning. The present work seeks to unravel how the readings of reality, highlighted above, can be applied to our inherited Christian history, going right back to the New Testament itself.

## Features of Postcolonialism

Postcolonialism, therefore, is the study of how power is transmitted, imposed, appropriated, and internalized, highlighting particularly the several subconscious factors that characterize that process. Over time several of the key features have become so normalized, institutionalized and validated – culturally, socially and religiously – their resilience seems almost unassailable. Those calling for a deeper critique will not merely be sidelined, they are also likely to encounter ridicule and ostracization. As Anne Schaef Wilson (1988) highlighted many years ago, the patriarchal power structures of our contemporary culture survive primarily through their addictive lure; at both the personal and institutional levels, addictions are never easy to dislodge, and will resist fiercely any attempts at redress or reform.

The literature of postcolonialism provides a more penetrating critique of the patriarchal philosophy of divide and conquer. In the present work (Chapter Four) I will trace the history of patriarchal power deep into prehistoric times – a trajectory I believe is necessary when applying postcolonial insight to the religious (and Christian) experience. Postcolonial scholarship tends to begin with the rise of colonization as exercised by European conquerors in the 19th and 20th centuries. And the insights they surface are then applied to earlier epochs such as the Christian era, the particular focus of the present work.

In conjunction with postmodernism, postcolonial literature often alludes to the inherited notion of the *metanarrative*, asserting that there is only one true way to describe reality, the power-perspective of the ruling class. In historical terms that one way translates into the monopoly of the conqueror or the colonizer. It articulates the imperial view, keen to keep all other perspectives suspended or suppressed. The power adopted by the ruling class(es) to convince other classes that their interests are the interests of all, is often described as the *hegemony* of the imperial caste. In the past, such imperialism was reinforced by the notion of the divine right of kings, and the corollary that all imperial power is divinely mandated. The monotheistic religions (Judaism, Christianity, Islam) consistently exhibit this desire to monopolize. Even in India, the BJP party promotes the Hindu religion along similar lines, marking quite a departure from Hinduism's long tradition of a tolerant, inclusive faith system.

*Mapping* is the word used by postcolonialists to describe how colonizers delineated global space to create many of the prevailing boundaries that define nation states today. Nearly all modern nations were carved out of violence and warfare, creating cultural entities of a highly artificial nature with little bioregional or ecological congruence. And in many cases, monotheistic religions have supported and continue to endorse the violent and artificial construct. Currently, the Islamic religion is to the fore in this regard, while the Jewish-Christian (read: American) collusion around the State of Israel is one of the more blatant contemporary examples.

Within the delineated spaces, status of being in or out has to be clearly established. In postcolonial theory, *alterity* is the word used to describe the state of being other or different, identifying those excluded from the mainstream culture because the inclusion of such groups or persons is deemed to be a threat to the integrity (read: power) of the dominating group. However, alterity carries a more complex connotation when adopted by minority groups seeking integration and acceptance within a dominant culture. And this is where the notion of *ambivalence* comes into play. The colonizer may view the colonized as inferior yet exotically other, while the colonized may simultaneously admire and hate the colonizer. Fundamentalist religious groups often exhibit this contradictory behavior.

Postcolonialism shares with mainstream Christianity a strong concern for the poor and marginalized, expressed in the frequently used term: *the subaltern*. However, for Gayatri Chakravorty Spivak, the term is used to refer to all groups that fall outside any official history or system of representation. It seems important to imperial domination to name and highlight a significant other(s) on to whom it can project its negative and derogatory perceptions, and onto whom it can displace blame to exonerate its own performance. Classically this leads to *scapegoating*, a dominant feature of all patriarchal societies, one that has received only scant attention in postcolonial literature. A frequently noted response of subalterns is that of collusion with the very powers they seek to erode or transform. *Mimicry* is the word used to describe this feature, described by Bhabha (1994, 84, 96):

> Mimicry is an emerging phenomenon in the middle of the process of conflating cultures between the colonizer and the colonized in that the colonized subject is reproduced as "almost the same, but not quite" as the colonizer. . . . When the colonized follows and resembles the colonizer's culture, behavior, and thought, the copying of the colonized turns out to be both mockery and menace to the colonizers.

This is an intriguing and complex notion, quite similar to *internalized oppression* – indicating that in the very process of resisting the oppression of the colonizer, the colonized end up adapting language, customs, and behaviors of those they seek to expel. Postcolonial scholars engaging New Testament research highlight several examples of mimicry within the New Testament writings, while the scripture scholar, Kathleen Corley (2002) avers that Jesus himself fell foul of colonial mimicry.

*Language* is the subject of much postcolonial critique, how subtly and deviously we use language not merely to subjugate and control but to validate and justify a range of imperial behaviors. When the then-American president, George W. Bush, decided to attack Afghanistan in 2001, he proclaimed that war was necessary to procure peace, and named the invasion as *Operation Enduring Freedom*. In ecclesiastical terms we experience the debacle of the new missal introduced by the Catholic Church in 2011-2012. The stated intention was to reclaim the primacy of Latin as the liturgical language of the Church, but the undercurrent of imposing sameness as a mechanism of control was obvious to Catholics all over the English speaking world.

Finally, colonial studies give considerable attention to the plight of the millions displaced and scattered amid the social turmoil and political instability of the modern world. Some of the cultural dislocation seems to result from the aftereffects of colonial invasion. The term *diaspora* describes the voluntary or enforced migration of peoples from their native homelands. It is the plight of millions in the modern world. It raises a number of concerns around core identity, explored in the literature under the term *essentialism*. In several contemporary situations, precise identity is difficult to establish and this feels threatening to both colonizer and colonized alike.

Of particular concern is the ensuing *hybridity*, a term liberally used in postcolonial discourse. Hybridity refers principally to the creation of dynamic mixed cultures, a trend often dismissed by religionists as syncretism, with accompanying concern for racial and religious purity. In sociology and anthropology, hybrids were often seen as an aberration, worse than the inferior races, a weak and diseased mutation. In religious terms there is fear that everything could collapse into insipid relativism - an allegation frequently made by Pope Benedict XVI as a defense against inter-religious dialogue.

In postcolonial studies, hybridity no longer is solely associated with migrant populations and with border towns, it also applies contextually to the flow of cultures and their interactions. It describes new trans-cultural groupings that arise from cross-cultural exchange, exploring both positive and negative outcomes. Using the literature and other cultural expressions of colonial peoples, Homi Bhabha (1986) introduced an additional interpretation. He saw hybridity as a transgressive act challenging the colonizers' authority, values and representations and thereby constituting an act of self-empowerment and defiance.

## Key Names

For readers who wish to explore the scholarly background to postcolonial studies, or the more specific application to Christian faith, I outline briefly some of the outstanding names, cited in most of the literature.

*Frantz Fanon* (1925–1961) was a Martinique-born French psychiatrist, philosopher, revolutionary, and writer whose work is influential in the fields of postcolonial studies, critical theory and Marxism. He is a frequently cited pioneer of what we might now call postcolonial consciousness. Educated in the University of Lyon (in France) he is better known for his role in the Algerian struggle for independence and became a member of the Algerian National Liberation Front. His life and works have incited and inspired anti-colonial liberation movements for more than four decades. He is controversially known for his advocacy of violence in order to move beyond the colonial mindset. But violence in Fanon, who was trained as a psychoanalyst, is a cathartic practice aimed at 'cleansing' the male colonized psyche from the effects of the epistemic violence of colonialism. That is why Fanon supported the most violent factions of FLN in Algeria. It is important to read Fanon's emphasis on revolutionary violence within the discourse of psychoanalysis.

*Edward Said* (1935-2003). Said, one of the founding figures of postcolonialism, is named in every major text on the topic. He was a Columbia University professor and outspoken Palestinian activist, and of course, *Orientalism* (published in 1978) is his single best known written work in which he describes a subtle and persistent Eurocentric prejudice against Arab-Islamic peoples and their cultures. According to Said (1978), all existing written history of European colonial rule and political domination over the East is distorted and false, and he concludes that Western writers always depict the Orient as an irrational, weak, feminized '*other*', as compared to the rational, strong, masculine West. His other important works include *The World, the Text, the Critic* (1983), and *Culture and Imperialism* (1993).

Edward W. Said's *Orientalism* provides a piercing critique on how colonizers view colonized territories and cultures long after the colonizers had actually left. Looking in particular at the representations of Egypt and the Middle East in a variety of written materials, Said claims that Western researchers rarely tried to gather firsthand information from indigenous sources. Instead they made observations based upon commonly held assumptions about 'the Orient' as a mythic place of exoticism, moral laxity, and sexual degeneration. Often these unexamined assumptions became the basis of scientific truths which then functioned as a justification for the perpetuation of colonial values. Thus the colonial mind-set continues to perpetuate itself. (For useful critique of Said's work, see McLeod 2010, 56-67).

*Gayatri Chakravorty Spivak* was born in 1942 in Calcutta, India. Her academic base as a professor of literature was Columbia University (USA). She is best known for the essay "Can the Subaltern Speak?", considered a founding text of postcolonialism in which she first outlined the concept of the *subaltern*, referring to marginalized groups and lower classes who have been rendered without *agency* because of their social or historical status. Stephen Morton (2007) provides a fine overview of her life and thinking.

*Homi K. Bhabha* born in Mumbai, India in 1949 is Professor of English and American Literature at Harvard University. He is one of the most important figures in contemporary post-colonial studies, and has coined a number of the field's neologisms and key concepts, such as hybridity, mimicry, difference, ambivalence. In his best known work, *The Location of Culture* (1994), Bhabha introduces a subfield called *colonial discourse theory*, adding the concept of *ambivalence* (a psychological term meaning that among colonized subjects, there is the simultaneous existence of a complicit and resistant state of mind). Bhabha believes that ambivalence may be the single most important factor contributing to the eventual dissolution of colonialism and imperialism.

*R. S. Sugirtharajah* is generally recognized as a leading advocate of postcolonial analysis of the New Testament. Professor of Biblical hermeneutics at Birmingham University in the UK, he was born in Sri Lanka and had his postgraduate education in India and the UK. He is author and editor of significant volumes on biblical studies; among the better known are *Postcolonial Criticism and Biblical Interpretation* (2002) and *A Postcolonial Commentary on the New Testament Writings* (2009). His work ranges across many disciplinary borders and has been translated into Spanish, Italian, Japanese and Malay. Among his editorial responsibilities, he is the Editor for the Bible and Postcolonialism series, published by Continuum.

*Musa W. Dube,* a lecturer in religious and biblical studies at the University of Botswana, is best known for her written works: *Postcolonial Feminist Interpretation of the Bible* (2000) and editor of *Postcolonial Feminist Interpretation of the Bible* (2012). She combines her academic research with intense social activism around AIDS/HIV and gender oppression, particularly in African cultures.

Among the other scholars offering a postcolonial critique of the N.T. are Warren Carter, John D. Crossan, Richard Horsley, Tat-siong Benny Liew, Stephen D. Moore, Mary Ann Tolbert – names that occur frequently throughout this book. Additionally, theologians, such as Catherine Keller, Kwok Pui Lan, Marion

Grau and Joerg Rieger are beginning to apply postcolonial insight to a range of theological topics.

## Empire and the Postcolonial

The notion of *Empire* features in several fields of contemporary study. It is described by anti-globalization activist, David Korten (2006, 20), as ". . .a label for the hierarchical ordering of human relationships based on the principle of domination. The imperial mindset favors material surplus for the ruling classes, honors the dominator power of death and violence, denies the feminine principle, and suppresses realization of the potentials of human maturity." To which the scripture scholar, John Dominic Crossan (2007, 36) adds this astute and disturbing observation: "To resist empire as such we must know what we're up against. It is something inherent in civilization itself. Non-imperial civilization is something yet to be seen upon our earth."

In the egalitarian spirit of the 21st century, abetted by a growing sense of a more inter-connected world, millions aspire to a non-imperial way of living. This is a new moment in human civilization, in which a range of subtle forces seek to overthrow imperial hegemony. Overtly, this may manifest as an open disregard for all patriarchal institutions and their modes of hierarchical governance. Of course, those who invest heavily in such institutions will counter the anti-institutional rhetoric as a prescription for anarchy. This is precisely the reason why the new egalitarians tend to disregard the prevailing norms rather than seek to reform them. Subconsciously, they tend to behave more like Petrim Sorokin's "internal barbarians" who according to Sorokin (1957) tend to be the catalysts for cultural and historical breakthroughs.

Describing the goal of British imperialism in the 18-19th centuries, Denis Judd writes: "No one can doubt that the desire for profitable trade, plunder and enrichment was the primary force that led to the establishment of the imperial structure." (quoted in McLeod, 2010, 8). Rather than meet violence with more violence, the new egalitarians seek the way of non-violence (Kurlansky 2006; Rynne 2008). Among other things this involves withholding energy, and investing it in alternative strategies that birth a different reality. For the dominant culture, this looks like a cop-out. But it can have a counter-cultural potential instigating a shift of consciousness that in time can lead to new action and more empowering structures. Action follows thought – and as more people withdraw or withhold creative energy from the cult of imperialism – this non-violent, counter-intuitive option may be more promising than it initially appears.

Modern globalization presents the single greatest challenge today, for those who seek alternatives to our dominant imperial culture. With so much slick advertising, legal protection provided by imperial institutions like the WTO, and the prospect of lucrative gains (with scant attention to ecological or even personal well-being), mega-corporations rule the world, reaping havoc on indigenous enterprises and earthly resources on a vast scale. Today, the imperial power is in the corporations and not in nations or state-sponsored bodies. And humans have yet to develop the kinds of networks through which the corporations can be challenged and called to render accountability: to national governments, to people, and to the living earth itself.

The transformation of imperial power – into something more generic and empowering – is a long hazardous road. Postcolonialism, more than any other field of study, names many of the insidious elements, exposes the forces of corrupting power, unmasks the devious and dangerous games that uphold such power, and proffer an alternative vision for a more liberating and empowering future.

In the present work, the postcolonial critique of empire will be applied primarily to the Christian gospels and how contemporary Christians seek to live out their Gospel-based faith. To that end, Scripture scholar, R.S. Sugirtharajah (2002, 43-73) outlines six different methods to analyze and re-vision a postcolonial appropriation of Christian faith for our time.

1. *Dissident Reading*, creating a forum where the voices of the oppressed can be heard, their pain exposed, and their oppression confronted. In the present work, I will attempt to reclaim such a voice for those whose truth is either suppressed or undermined in Gospel lore. I often use poetry to access and restore the subverted voice.

2. *Resistant Reading*. In the time of Jesus many people resisted Roman imperialism and Jewish oppression, but the later Christian Church, adopting a dualistic split between religion and politics often failed to acknowledge the resistant voices.

3. *Heritagist Reading*. This strategy has been described as an attempt to retrieve cultural memory from amnesia caused by colonial oppression. How to reclaim customs, rituals, oral traditions, etc. from the past that can sustain people now in their desire to transcend the residue of colonial oppression. My attempt in Chapter Five to reclaim the deeper truths that may have been embedded in the Aramaic language adopts this strategy.

4. *Nationalist Reading*. Reasserting national sovereignty and indigenous integrity, to offset the invasive impact of the foreigner. Additionally, we also need to consider afresh those forms of national patriotism which can undermine rather than advance true freedom.

5. *Liberation Reading.* Discerning more deeply what true freedom means, and how to structure it in empowering ways for those who have been colonized – which today, must include the living earth as well as all the sentient creatures inhabiting our home planet. This strategy is the most frequently adopted throughout the present work.

6. *Dissentient Reading.* Seeks to highlight the subjectivity of minorities, those who can easily be neglected even in the throes of a new freedom. Women and children are the oft cited examples. They carry some of the worst wounds of warfare and conflict, but in the recovery period rarely obtain either the psychological, social or financial resources needed to regain a basic sense of normalcy and wholeness.

In the past, mainline religion (including Christianity) regarded such involvement as a dangerous distraction from the things of God, and from the salvation made possible through faith in God alone. Today, religion itself is central to the critique, particularly in its several deviations of bolstering and supporting the corruption of power. And those devious elements go right back to the time of Jesus himself- as I shall illustrate in subsequent chapters.

# Chapter 3:
## *Postcolonialism in the 21st century: Martha's Story.*

*As an Asian woman critic, I am painfully aware that the contemporary mental and intellectual space is controlled by the cultural hegemony of the West, the white gaze, and the increasing self-representation of the male.*

Kwok Pui-Lan.

*Often what is called 'mystery', is mere mystification, used to camouflage the power drives of those who don't want to be questioned.*

Catherine Keller.

Throughout the 1990s, I worked in London (UK) as a counselor to people with AIDS/HIV. I began the work under the dark cloud of an impending plague, reinforced by the fact that I spent my first three years accompanying people dying of AIDS-related illnesses. In those early days, when visiting clients in a hospital, we had to don special plastic uniforms, initially from head to foot, such was the irrational fear that this illness might be contagious.

In 1993 the first retroviral drugs entered the UK, specifically one known as AZT. Despite some early hitches, and some very disturbing symptoms for the recipients, the drugs proved effective, and people began outliving the morbid prognostications. By the end of the 1990s, throughout the entire Western world we had millions of people, diagnosed as HIV+ but living quite normal lives – as long as they also kept vigilance on stress levels, good diet, etc.

The fear of the impending plague quickly evaporated – for Westerners, but not elsewhere in the world. The horror stories formerly associated with the West, now began to emerge from Africa. Whole families, even entire communities, succumbed to the deadly illness. As for the retroviral drugs, the people of Africa simply could not afford them, and pharmaceutical companies are not renowned for their altruistic spirit. Money comes first, not people's lives.

## Martha's Death and Resurrection.

In 2003, I was facilitating some workshops in Lusaka, Zambia. With my background experience in AIDS-HIV work, I felt I could handle Martha's story without too much emotional trauma. I had been given all the facts, the grim details of Martha's ten year ordeal during which she had buried all her eight offspring, all their spouses, and two of her grandchildren. She was now left caring for *thirty grandchildren*, varying in age from 18 to 2 years old.

I met her in a large dilapidated hall, her brow etched with age (she was only 62), anguish and sorrow. I felt so petrified and insecure. What do I say to this woman? What can one say? Words came forth - I am not sure from where: "How do you cope?" "What keeps you going?"

Her response was quick, clear, and even assertive. She pointed to a big crucifix on the wall – a Mel Gibson-type tortured Jesus, serrated flesh and dripping in blood. "Thank God he died for me," she said, "because without him and his cross I certainly could not carry mine." Angela, one of her supporters, intervened assuring me of Martha's deep devotion to the crucifix, and how such devotion empowers and sustains her in her dreadful ordeal. Eighteen times morning and night, Martha knelt in front of her crucifix at home, and devoutly kissed it as she remembered her eighteen loved ones who have been taken by AIDS-HIV.

Of course, it crossed my mind, that among her remaining 30 grandchildren are several who are HIV infected (maybe all are) and it is only a matter of time till they too succumb to the illness, followed by an untimely death. Martha will have more funerals – and she will need to add extra kisses to her crucifix morning and night.

Perhaps, it was people like me, who had met one or other of the several Marthas around Africa that eventually could no longer tolerate the painful injustice of millions living in the West because they could afford the retroviral drugs, and millions dying in Africa because they could not afford them. Something had to be done – and it appeared that those with money and power would not take the initiative.

So, there emerged a group of angry, transgressive activists. They began manufacturing retroviral drugs – initially in India and then along the Eastern African seaboard. They had effectively robbed the copyright (the patent) from the pharmaceutical companies. They knew the pharmaceutical companies were protected by the laws and procedures of the WTO (World Trade Organization), and they knew the huge risks they were taking with their lives and their safety. With hindsight, it seems they got away with it.

Today, retroviral drugs are readily available throughout Africa, and at a price the people can afford. Countries such as Uganda and South Africa are already reporting declining rates in those dying of the virus. And most amazing of all, Martha has had no more funerals since I met her on that memorable day in July 2003.

## From Consolation to Liberation

Martha's story is a postcolonial parable for the 21st century, one that the historical Jesus would certainly tell if he were around today. It gets right to the core of postcolonial evangelization and the formidable challenges that ensue.

During her ten years of grief and trauma, Martha needed her devotions for both strength and consolation. She needed her crucifix to keep her going, maybe even to enable her to get out of bed and face each awful day. She also prayed the Rosary every day and beseeched God with several novenas. And she kept doing it, despite the fact that God never seemed to answer.

Martha's faith belongs to what I will describe as the *Devotion of Consolation*. Throughout the ages, it has sustained and empowered millions of believers, including my own faith in my younger years. It seeks to bombard God for clemency and mercy. It works on the conviction that the more we multiply devotional practices, such as prayers and novenas, the stronger the likelihood that God will respond. And if God doesn't respond, there is a kind of psychological satisfaction that one has done everything one could have done. It may be described as a devotion of desperation.

However, we must recognize its effectiveness. It does sustain and empower the Marthas of this world, and there are millions of such people, not merely in cultures of poverty and oppression, but located throughout the entire planet. Without such devotion, millions would succumb to anomie and despair. It may be a Marxist opiate of the people or a Freudian infantile illusion, but it is a crucially important asset to retain meaning and sanity for those victimized by the cruel injustices that envelop our world today.

Christians, and others, recognize Martha's need for the devotion of consolation, but are becoming increasingly suspicious of its dysfunctional and disempowering impact. And this is where the postcolonial critique assumes central importance. All the gazing on earth at the crucifix, all the energy involved in beseeching God, could never have delivered the freedom and empowerment that Martha now knows, thanks to the brave and risky activists who broke WTO laws to procure cheap drugs for the suffering people of Africa. What the activists achieved, I wish to describe as the *Spirituality of Liberation*. And it was that empowering spirituality, and not the devotion of consolation that made the breakthrough possible for Martha and for millions like her.

Martha's story vividly demonstrates the pervasive and enduring resilience of colonization. It blatantly illustrates the racist oppression of black by white long after European colonization ceased. And it unmasks the brutal face of *modern globalization,* unrelentingly addicted to the power of money. At a more personal level it reveals the indoctrination of colonial religiosity, with the delusory and disempowering influence it can have, holding millions of disenfranchised people in its co-dependent grip.

## Devotion: Postcolonial Critique

Without devotional prayer with which millions of disenfranchised people plead to God on a daily basis, life would be so brutal and intolerable as to make existence impossible for many. Dysfunctional though such behavior is, we need such pseudo-spiritual outlets. *How to use them constructively and proactively – to bring about systemic and political change – is the challenge posed by a postcolonial critique.* And firstly, that requires us to undertake a more penetrating analysis to expose the paralyzing power of such devotional practices. People whose faith-practice revolves around this quality of devotion tend to exhibit the following dispositions:

- They have internalized a poor self-image, with unworthiness as a dominant emotion. Their sense of unworthiness may be reinforced by exaggerated guilt or shame about past sins or transgressions. Being a good enough person is simply never good enough.

- Their God-image tends to be that of a distant, fearful, judging deity, whom they are forever trying to pacify (as a compensation for their perceived unworthiness), and whose favor they feel they have to invoke over and over again.

- Their strategy for invoking the ruling God is that of repetitious prayers, usually adopting forms they have learned in childhood and have retained unreflectively for much of their adult lives.

- Such people are the victims of a subtle but pervasive patriarchal, colonial ploy that seeks to control people by keeping them passive and subdued. By consistently reminding people of their unworthiness, their sins and failures, it becomes much easier to subjugate their wills and manipulate their behavior.

- In several cases, these people take into adult life everything they learned and internalized as children. Their faith rarely matures into a more adult sense of spiritual engagement.

- Individual salvation – as applied to the soul, and not to the whole person – is the primary goal of this religiosity. It is highly anthropocentric – such religion has nothing to do with the non-human realms of life.

- The colonizing forces advocate suffering for the sake of suffering as a primary, authentic spiritual disposition. Embracing suffering (the Cross), and enduring it with passive resignation, is deemed more authentic than taking steps to alleviate it.

- The ultimate goal is proclaimed as one of escape from this vale of tears to the fulfillment and happiness of a life hereafter. The present creation tends to be viewed as hopelessly flawed – usually perceived to be the consequence of original sin.

- In this cultural and religious construct, faith in Jesus is heavily influenced by Atonement Theory. Jesus is the only one who can redeem people from sin - and guarantee their salvation in a life hereafter.

- Such subdued, colonized people have very little interest in the Bible. Scripture is for priests, rather than for people; to be used for preaching and teaching, rather than being viewed as a resource for daily life. The priest tends to be regarded as God's perfect representative on earth.

- Allegiance to Church is viewed primarily as the fulfillment of obligations. Church authority is often vested with a pseudo-divine significance. Attendance at Church services, rather than participation in them, is what really matters.

- Clergy often laud this quality of religiosity as "the simple faith of the simple people," a condescending, patronizing appraisal that signals clearly the clergy's own desire to dominate and control.

- When people drift away from this quality of religiosity – as tends to happen when their material conditions improve – they often drift aimlessly. Devotional practices will wane, only to be rapidly invoked should a personal or family crisis arise. In modern Catholicism, there is also some evidence indicating a transition from a devotional sense of faith to alignment with modern Pentecostal worship.

- The colonization therefore is thorough and deeply ingrained. Occasionally, one encounters people who, in daily life, act with competence and remarkable levels of creativity and responsibility, but when it comes to religious practice they fall into a kind of religious trance, largely devoid of the reflection and adult maturity they exhibit in every other area of their lives.

- Transformative growth into more informed, adult ways of faith-engagement may never happen, and when it does transpire, it is likely to be initially dislocating, and will require consistent reassurance over a long period of time.

Despite this comprehensive critique of devotional practices, I do not advocate the abolition of popular devotions. I respectfully acknowledge how crucially important such devotions are for the sheer survival of people like Martha, who tragically constitute a sizeable proportion of today's human population. To try and get rid of such devotional religiosity would actually reinforce rather than undermine colonial power. The challenge facing all religions today is how to re-appropriate and re-integrate devotional practices, placing them at the service of more generic and empowering outcomes for person and planet alike. What this means will become clearer as we illuminate the spiritual and theological significance of the *Spirituality of Liberation.*

## Liberation: Postcolonial Empowerment

The *devotion of consolation* denotes a set of dispositions whereby the colonizing forces have you where they want you to be: firmly under their thumb! Good subservient devotees who will not ask any awkward questions and will play the patriarchal game in faithful obedience to a God - largely construed in the image and likeness of the patriarchs themselves. To one degree or another, every religion has adopted this strategy – we'll see why in Chapter Four.

Meanwhile, every age has had its religious counter-culture, and arguably every major religion has an underlying empowering authenticity, usually buried beneath several layers of colonial imposition. In the mid-twentieth century millions of Christians – and adherents of other religious systems as well – awoke to a shift in religious awareness. It might best be explained as an evolutionary awakening that caught up with millions of people all over the world. People began to question as never before – and this time, they did not feel guilty about doing so. People threw off the shackles of a religion that no longer felt right – and intuitively realized that it was okay to do so. People began to think for themselves, ask questions one time reserved to revered clerics, and dispute religious issues for which one would be condemned to hell just a few years earlier. The *spirituality of liberation* was rebirthed afresh.

Throughout the closing decades of the twentieth century the *spirituality of liberation* morphed into several new constructs, some of the best known being: liberation theology, feminist spirituality, creation-centered faith, multi-faith dialogue, Basic Christian Communities, mystical explorations (often with a strong Eastern flavor). The *Spirituality of Liberation* came to be identified by the following central features:

- The need to transcend and outgrow all dualistic splitting particularly the binary opposition of the sacred v. secular. All dualisms were perceived as patriarchal ploys necessary to reinforce the philosophy of divide-and-conquer.

- The ability to empower became a primary criterion of authentic faith and religion. In the Christian context this led to an extensive re-appropriation of the Gospel notion of *the Kingdom of God* (more in Chapter Five), often resulting in down-playing the significance of formal Churches, a tension that prevails to the present day.

- All patriarchal constructs were questioned and critiqued. Many people became suspicious of the exercise of top-down hierarchal systems and yearned for strategies and structures more conducive to dialogue and collaboration, empowerment and liberation.

- People began to join networks, and form new coalitions from the ground up, eschewing where possible control from on high. Many such groups became highly subversive (e.g, the activists who reproduced the retroviral drugs at a price Africans could afford to pay). The American social researcher, Paul Hawken (2007), provides a comprehensive overview of the power of networking.

- Patronizing charity was critically reviewed. Justice-before-charity became a new liberating faith-focus, another issue still evolving in the emerging religious consciousness of our time.

45

- Religious practice (prayer and liturgy) lost pride of place to practical strategies devoted to building a better world characterized by justice, equality, peace and right living.

- Growing suspicion arose around doctrinal and dogmatic teachings, once again viewed as ploys to reinforce the truth of power rather than the power of truth.

- Adult Faith Development began to emerge as being more important and potentially more empowering than the catechesis of youth. (More in O'Murchu 2010; 2013).

- Spiritual accompaniment (often called Spiritual Direction) evolved from being a clerical monopoly to a resource extensively used and promoted by lay people – particularly in the West.

- A kind of religious recklessness was widely noted, as people spontaneously disconnected from former indoctrination, and sometimes opted for 'new age' alternatives. This move has often been heavily criticized as excessively individualistic, frequently, underestimating new affiliations that ensued around justice-making and social action (networking).

- More people began to differentiate childhood indoctrination from adult appropriation in matters of faith and morals. The option to outgrow what they had internalized as children often proved – and still does prove – to be emotionally and spiritually dislocating. To resolve the inner tension, some opted to abandon religion entirely.

- Individual salvation – as applied to the soul, and not to the whole person – lost much of its inherited appeal. Intuitively, more people realized that salvation as growth-in-wholeness (holiness) required engagement in every domain of life, and not exclusively in the human realm.

The *Spirituality of Liberation* does not fit into any conventional political or religious philosophy. It is the vision of free spirits, fiercely committed to protest, justice, equality, empowerment, concerned not merely with the plight of suffering people but also the exploited earth itself. Many of its more overt advocates are not particularly religious (in terms of allegiance to any one formal religion) but are clearly inspired and animated by spiritual values. In Christian terms, they relate minimally with the Church, but believe passionately in the New Reign of God, under its more modern renaming as the *Companionship of Empowerment* (more in Chapter Five). For such people the crucial issue is *orthopraxy*, and not *orthodoxy*.

## Integrating Devotion and Liberation

Can the two strands meet? Is integration possible? I answer affirmatively, and I offer the following example from the city of Manila in the Philippines.

Close to Manila International airport is the Catholic Church of Baclaran, home to the National Shrine of our Lady of Perpetual Help. Every Wednesday, an estimated 100,000 Filipinos come to the Church to participate in the Novena and the accompanying devotions. Many of these are poor people, some from Manila's famous squatter area of Tondo, located approximately 10 kilometers from Baclaran.

The Church (and Shrine) is run by the Redemptorist Congregation, a Religious Order devoted to preaching the plentiful redeeming love of God especially for the poor and socially deprived. Thousands of the same people come to Baclaran Church every Wednesday and participate fully in the devotions. Many have been coming for several years, and little has changed in their personal lives or material circumstances. The prayer and devotion sustains them in their daily and life-long struggles, but does it help to change their oppressive degrading plight?

The poor people of Tondo flock to Baclaran Church. Tondo is a sprawling squatter camp, home to some 300,000 people living in squalid conditions of dire poverty and some of the most dehumanizing conditions to be observed anywhere on planet earth. Baclaran Church offers hope to the people of Tondo, the kind of hope that keeps them going from one day to the next, and from one crisis to the next. It mediates comfort and consolation but offers nothing to challenge the people's oppression, and empower the people to demand greater justice, and some semblance of true freedom. Paradoxically, the community at Baclaran could stand accused of reinforcing the people's poverty and maintaining their co-dependency with the political and social forces of oppression.

Let's imagine, the Redemptorist Order opting for a prophetic empowering response to the plight of those living in Tondo. Let's explore a scenario whereby the Redemptorists would begin to confront local government and offer to liaise with an agency like *Habitat for Humanity* to build some decent housing for the people of Tondo. A strategy, informed with prophetic imagination (cf, Brueggemann 1978, 1984) might unfold like this: The people would gather as usual for Wednesday's devotions in Baclaran Church, but on each subsequent Wednesday the Redemptorists would invite and challenge those same people to go instead to Tondo, and engage with Habitat for Humanity in building houses for the local people. Instead of using the popular devotions for their own personal holiness and salvation, the participants would be invited to transfer their devotional energy to the good of the deprived people of Tondo. *Devotion* would serve to fuel and support *Liberation*.

Most likely, such a strategy would eventually require a restructuring of the devotions themselves so that the devotional ingredients (gestures, language, prayers, etc.) enhance and sustain the work and toil involved in upgrading the living standards of the people of Tondo. The devotional focus would have shifted from desperate appeals to a desperate God - to work some miracle for the plight of the poor, to a collaborative endeavor of people co-creating with God to facilitate new hope and meaning. It could result in revolutionary changes on several aspects of people's faith life and a radical shift in their understanding of popular devotion.

Like all human examples, it falls short of a liberating ideal. The very suggestion that others do something for the people of Tondo – rather than empower them to be self-empowering – is an old colonial strategy that needs critical redress. It is, however, an inspiring example of what could transpire as an empowering collaborative endeavor – fully congruent with the charismatic vision of the Redemptorist Order, mediating "plentiful redemption." It highlights the potential for a new integration of devotion and liberation, while enhancing a deeper understanding of both elements. It builds bridges between people and social reality, straddles the dualistic split between the sacred and the secular, and calls forth a sense of Christian accountability far more congruent with the Gospel vision of the Kingdom of God.

Without consciously naming or exposing oppressive undercurrents, it aims to end and transform some of the insidious colonial forces, keeping the poor trapped in abject poverty on the one hand, and in a disempowering popular religiosity, on the other hand. The proposal opens the possibility of several transformative breakthroughs, in a collaborative endeavor that is political, economic, social, religious, theological and deeply personal all at once. It is the ultimate dream of every postcolonial critique.

## Gospel Liberation

In concluding this Chapter, I return to Martha's story and connect with seminal Gospel stories to reinforce Martha's empowering breakthrough. We begin with the best known Martha of Gospel lore, grieving the death of her brother Lazarus (Jn.11:1-44). In the loaded symbolism of John's Gospel we must not waste time striving to discern the supernatural power whereby Jesus revives a corpse of four days old. Most commentators allude to the Resurrection context of this story, a parable rich in metaphor and overstatement on the life-force that defies all forms of meaningless or untimely death. And indeed, might it be, as Cynthia Bourgeault (2008) suggests that Martha and Mary are two aspects (sub-personalities, if you wish) of the Gospel's supreme hospice-caregiver, namely *Mary Magdalene*. Like the broken-hearted Martha I met in Zambia, not yet the recipient of Resurrection hope, so too, Magdalene eventually came to a Resurrection breakthrough, but only after she had endured the ignominious heart-break of Calvary. In postcolonial spirituality, meaningless death must never be allowed to have the final word, nor must insipid devotions ever be allowed to hinder the breakthrough to which every free being is entitled.

Three other Gospel stories illustrate the transition from the devotion of consolation to the spirituality of liberation. Firstly, the story of *the widow's mite,* secondly *the woman bent over,* and thirdly *the woman who confronts the unjust judge.* In all three cases we have had centuries of devout commentaries lauding the women for personal holiness and devoted suffering in the service of duty. Postcolonialism sees them in a very different light: as powerful parabolic figures calling patriarchal oppression to transparency and to a more empowering form of accountability. And in all three cases the empowering breakthrough resonates more coherently in poetry than in prose.

Beginning with the story of *the widow's mite,* let's note the context in which both Mark and Luke place this story (Mk.12:41-44; Lk. 21:1-4), between the denunciation of the Pharisees for "taking advantage of widows and robbing them of their homes," and the denunciation of the temple (cf. Lk. 21:5ff; Mk.13:1ff). Ched Myers (1988, 321) reads the story as a primary example of subversive speech, calling the hearer's attention to the pernicious way in which the Temple robs even a poor widow of the little she has left to live on. (Also Addison G. Wright 1982). The Korean scholar, Seong Hee Kim (2010, 79-99), views the story as a rupturing of the imperial system, exposing the cruel lengths to which patriarchal power will go, in its greed to dominate and control.

Conventional exegeses for far too long admired the widow's generosity of spirit, giving all she had from the little she had left over, a devotional model of the long-suffering martyr, a sacrificial victim of true discipleship. Such an interpretation leaves the imperial system off the hook, and leaves their corruption unnamed and unexamined. The widow is not an ideal Christian to be emulated for all she sacrifices, but a subversive example of colonial oppression buttressed by religious devotionalism.

*Robbing even a Widow's Mite!*

*She's oft admired by homilists for giving all she had.*
*And allegedly she gave it all, her mite to mighty God.*
*And we're told the Temple treasury was the focus of her giving,*
*And it sounds like they don't give a damn what she has left for living.*
*Having stripped her of all she had to placate some wicked God.*

*We need to give discerning care to the context of the tale,*
*How widows oft are victimized and robbed of all their bail.*
*So cruel the mercy she must gain to win her way into God's reign.*
*No wonder Jesus pounces and the Temple fierce denounces,*
*For robbing her of all she had to placate some wicked God.*

*Suspicion's hermeneutic we need at times employ,*
*'Cos holy writ's corruption can be devious and sly.*
*And care to take collude we not, with crippling guilt and fear,*
*That have no place in God's New Reign, new life and hope declare.*
*And retrieve the widow's dignity from the Temple's wicked God.*

## The Woman Bent Over

The story of *the woman bent over* is recorded in Lk.13:10-17. In the time of Jesus it was common to attribute illness to the influence of evil spirits. Metaphorically, however, the Roman occupation and interference in the land of Israel can also be understood as a form of demonic possession, a postcolonial dynamic employed by Mark in the story of the Gerassean demoniac (5:1ff). Several allusions to loss of sight, hearing and speech might well have a similar significance: forms of paralysis ensuing from the psychosomatic internalization of oppression and fear, sometimes involving physical as well as psychological abuse. *Internalized oppression* is often considered to be the cause and source of such physical and emotional ailments.

The story, therefore, becomes an attack on the prevailing devotionalism, and its paralyzing nature. Jesus reminds the synagogue leader that his religiosity allows for an animal to be fed and watered on the Sabbath, so why not attend to the healing needs of a woman oppressively entrapped for eighteen years? And as a daughter of Abraham, she is entitled to the rights of her faith for liberty and empowerment.

But is there not a more subversive subtext to this parabolic narrative? In the eyes of the dominant religion, women should know their subservient place and remain therein. It suits the system to have women (and other inferior people) afflicted by debilitating illnesses, and while she is bent over, it is not that easy to look her in the eye, nor can she easily catch the attentive eye of any other, least of all of her oppressors.

But now she is standing upright! What a shock that must have been for the synagogue official! How does an official cope with someone who for eighteen years has been effectively a non-person? Beyond the devotionalism by which she could so easily be dismissed, ignored and oppressed, she now stands upright in full sight of the official. He cannot but meet the gaze of her new-found freedom. The spirituality of liberation has truly set her free. It is difficult to contain the enthusiasm of poetry when confronted with such a daring breakthrough:

## *Standing Up Straight!*

*They thought 'twas the spirits inflicted her pain*
*With posture distorted she moved with great strain.*
*Bent over by burden for eighteen long years,*
*With anguish and struggle, and crippled by fear.*
*To stand straight again, being a woman in sin,*
*Was a dream she had never imagined!*

*And the culture of judgement she could not escape,*
*Some curse from the past they alleged for her fate.*
*So crushed in her spirit by a faith quite corrupt,*
*It took courage defiant to hold her chin up.*
*To stand straight again, in a culture of sin,*
*Was a dream she had never imagined.*

*And Jesus saw through the distortions so false,*
*A daughter of Abraham, she, too, had her place.*
*An equal in status to whatever the force,*
*And he called forth the freedom to dislodge her curse.*
*To stand straight again, in spite of her sin,*
*Was a dream she had never imagined.*

*The Spirit of life and the Spirit that heals,*
*Is the first touch of God to free and release.*
*The forces that bind through shame, guilt and fear,*
*Will never outdo God's freedom so clear.*
*To stand straight again, and outgrow her sin,*
*Was a dream she had never imagined.*

*But the Synagogue boss with his righteous acclaim,*
*Felt his power undermined by this freedom regained.*
*And a Sabbath good deed, it angered his soul,*
*While, in fact, he's annoyed by a woman made whole.*
*To stand straight again, in spite of her sin,*
*Was a dream that HE never imagined.*

*She stands in her place, her body aglow.*
*She raises her voice with the wisdom to know*
*That freedom begets a new option to grow,*
*With oppression declared to rule us no more.*
*To stand straight again, oppression upend,*
*Is the task for us all to imagine.*

When I first met Martha in Zambia she never looked directly at me. Her eyes were downcast for our entire conversation. The sadness of her expression was overtly depressing. Psychologically and physically she was a woman bent over! Six years later (in 2009), another Zambian colleague sent me a photo of Martha on the occasion of the confirmation ceremony of six of her grandchildren. I could scarcely believe it was the same woman I had encountered in 2003. She was elegantly dressed and her face was aglow with radiance and hope. The liberating words of scripture sprung straight to mind: "Unbind her and let her go free" – the freedom bequeathed through the empowering grace of the spirituality of liberation.

## Perseverance in Prayer.

Few stories in the Gospels evoke such unrelenting perseverance as that of the persistent widow (Lk.18:1-8). According to Jewish teaching, widows were to be respected as elders. However, being deprived of a significant male in their lives they were socially dismissed as non-persons. In a modern oppressive culture, they might be derogatorily advised to go and say their payers and prepare for a happy and holy death. Devotionalism is their due role, and they should behave accordingly.

William Herzog (1994, 225, 229ff) suggests that this parable is rife with paradox and reversal. All the roles are topsy-turvy. And the judge knows he has no choice but to condescend. This is a woman who has walked the long road to freedom and is not going to compromise her hard won gains. She seeks justice for herself and for all who have been disempowered by colonial oppression. She is an eminent disciple of the spirituality of liberation. And her story glows in the power of poetry:

## The Widow's Empowerment

*I'm a widow with small fortune and adversaries press hard*
*And with all my siblings buried, I'm alone.*
*I detect new liberation in the air,*
*A companionship empowering all who care*
*Confronting the corruption of despair.*
*I know things can be different, so I am holding out*
*Calling all corrupting forces to account.*

*The judicial system of this land is rotten to the core*
*The power-elite control the upper ground.*
*In my case, they will drag the verdict out*
*Time is on their side – of that I have no doubt*
*And their complicated rhetoric has clout.*
*I know things can be different, so I am holding out*
*Calling all corrupting forces to account.*

*I have long respected Torah and believe the power of truth*
*I expect this judge his faithfulness uphold.*

*I have a right to justice like the rest*
*Though I can't cite Holy Scripture to behest*
*I know that Holy Wisdom will assist.*
*Yes, I know things can be different, so I am holding out*
*Calling all corrupting forces to account.*

*The Companions of Empowerment bring vision to my soul*
*No force upon the earth can wear me down.*
*God's new empowering vision interrupts*
*The power-games whereby judgement oft corrupts,*
*I believe in the transgression that disrupts.*
*I know things can be different, so I am holding out*
*Calling all corrupting forces to account.*

However, in adapting this parable, it is the more explicit link with Martha's story I wish to highlight with its potential for postcolonial critique. The opening verse states that Jesus told the parable to encourage the disciples to pray incessantly and never be discouraged. V.7 picks up the same theme, describing such petitionary prayer as crying out to God day and night. Is this not the same prayer of desperation, invoked by Martha (in Zambia) and by the thousands who gather in the Baclaran Church every Wednesday? Is this the kind of co-dependent prayer that Jesus or God wants? Is it even congruent with other teachings on prayer highlighted in both the Old and New Testaments?

Jewish scholars such as Hermann Strack and Paul Billerbeck have assembled evidence which indicates that continuous prayer, in the Jewish mentality, would be obnoxious or annoying to God; according to Dan.6:10, three times a day was considered enough (cf. Hicks 1991, 213). Thus, Jesus' encouragement to pray *pantote* (continuously) must be seen in contrast with the contemporary Jewish attitude. It also marks a significant departure from the Sermon on the Mount where Christians are taught not to use many words in prayer, and stands in stark contrast to the parable of "The Pharisee and Tax Collector" (Lk.18:9-14), which denounces the one of many words and exalts the brief plea for mercy verbalized by the tax collector. Finally, let's also note St. Paul's admonition against many words, so that instead we can heed the Spirit who calls forth from deep within (Rom.8:26-27).

Who, therefore, is encouraging persistent prayer: Jesus, Luke, or a subsequent redactor of Luke's Gospel? Scripture scholar, Joachim Jeremias thinks that this can hardly be a correct indication of the aim of the parable (cf. Hicks 1991, 213). Rather, Luke seems to be writing so as to encourage his readers to pray for vindication with the knowledge that God will certainly grant it when the Son of Man comes again. Luke seems to be supporting an understanding of prayer more in tune with the devotion of consolation described earlier in this Chapter, whereas the parable in its original context might have a great deal more to do with the spirituality of liberation, and the establishment of justice for the marginalized and oppressed.

The central issue in the parable is the widow in pursuit of justice from a manipulative patriarchal judge, whose control is being challenged to the breaking point. At first the judge refuses, but then after a while gives in because he is afraid that he will be disgraced publicly. The parable, then, falls within the prophetic picture of the poor widow against the powerful, unrighteous judge. Not merely does the woman win because of her persistence, she also unmasks the systemic oppression, calling forth a new horizon for empowering justice and freedom for all.

The parable calls the judge to a new level of transparency, compassion and hope, leading to the liberating question for all who seek justice and empowering love: "Will not God vindicate his own people if his unrighteous judge vindicates the widow?" While it may seem as though God has forgotten his people, he will act on their behalf when the time comes. There is certainty with respect to God's ultimate victory in the coming of the Son of Man. However, uncertainty lies in whether the disciples will be as persistent as the widow was. Will the disciples follow the example of the widow – in radical and subversive fidelity to God's empowering vision? Will the Son of Man, when he comes, find faith upon the earth?

## Towards a Postcolonial Future

In Martha's tragic narrative, we encounter a devotion that is pragmatically sustaining, but spiritually and culturally paralyzing. Her liberating breakthrough is made possible by a spirituality that can integrate the sacred and the secular, and therefore challenge and outwit the oppressive forces of colonization. And those that made the breakthrough possible, transgressed several legally approved norms and guidelines – in the name of an empowering breakthrough that has all the hallmarks of Gospel liberation.

For all formal religions, this breakthrough story presents daunting challenges. The story serves as a perennial postcolonial parable challenging religious believers (of every persuasion) firstly, to become more aware of religion's long history of complicity with patriarchal power, and secondly to differentiate more clearly between a spirituality that feeds co-dependency as distinct from one that foments empowering liberation.

Martha's story provides an exemplary narrative within which all the major religions can engage with the critical questions raised by a postcolonial critique. How do we enable people to name and confront what hinders or undermines the realization of their God-given potentialities, and how does religion itself reinforce and validate the forces which bind and oppress? Without engaging such questions we cannot hope to unleash what promises liberating justice and religious empowerment for a different and better future.

Relevant and important though these questions are for all religions, I will devote the rest of this book to the Christian faith and its potential to deliver postcolonial breakthroughs. When we examine Christianity from this perspective we can glimpse more readily universal values and aspirations that are endorsed and supported by all major faiths. The deeper we go within one religious tradition, the greater the chances of unearthing what we hold in common as people endowed by the one universal Spirit of God.

# Chapter 4:
## *Colonial Rhetoric in New Testament Literature*

*Postcolonial criticism will continue to have purchase as long as the Bible contains three potent elements: conquest, conversion, and election, a heady mixture which has the potential to turn innocent, cultured and erudite men, yes, mainly men, into violent predators.*

R.S. Sugirtharajah

*Explaining the remarkable coherence and stability of the empire involves a complex and subtle set of interrelated factors, especially a remarkable interplay of religion and economics in the network of imperial power relations: the cult of the emperor in nearly every major city and province and the extensive pyramids of patronage relations.*

Richard Horsley.

The Sri Lankan biblical scholar, R.S. Sugirtharajah (2002; 2005; 2012) is an oft cited authority on postcolonialism in the New Testament. Fernando Segovia, Benny Liew, Stephen D. Moore and Kwok Pui-Lan are among the other leading names. Although not officially classified as postcolonialists, well known scholars such as John Dominic Crossan, Richard Horsley, Joerg Rieger and Elizabeth Schussler-Fiorenza address power related dynamics closely aligned to the postcolonial critique.

Of the aforementioned, Elizabeth Schussler-Fiorenza, more explicitly than others, highlights the patriarchal subtext of the Christian scriptures. In conjunction with other feminists, her concern is the sociological and structural elements of patriarchy, paying only minimal attention to its deeper historical and cultural roots. It seems to me that the origins of patriarchal domination, as we have experienced it throughout the past 2,000 years of Christendom, can be traced right back to the shadow side of the *agricultural revolution*, some 10,000 years ago. Why go that far back? And in dealing with such ancient material how does one establish rational fact from speculative construct?

## The Roots of Colonization

While lacking the fine detail that scholars rightly seek, we know a great deal about the agricultural revolution and the momentous cultural transition that ensued. The comprehensive study of Graeme Barker (2009) is immensely helpful in this regard.

Firstly, we need to clarify the nature of the revolution in question: it did not mark the discovery of agriculture – humans had been engaging with the fertility of the land for thousands of years previously – but the organization and stratification of agricultural activity. The commodification and functional use of the land became the central focus. Land was objectified as monetized usufruct. Therefore the more you had the wealthier you became. And if you needed more you either bargained to obtain it or acquired it by force. Thus we witness conflict over the land to a degree that does not seem to have been prevalent prior to that time.

This new relationship with the land marked a shift in consciousness, leading to what sociologist, Steve Taylor, describes as *an ego explosion*, or what mythologist, Joseph Campbell, called *the great reversal*. Taylor dates this novel cultural departure to about 6,000 years ago when a new ice-wave transformed North-Africa and Saudi Arabia (what Taylor calls *Saharasia*) from a rich fertile plain into the arid desert we know today. The interactive relationship with the soil, more characteristic of the hunter-gatherer phase, was abruptly disrupted, pitting the human against the land, and leading males particularly into a new mode of relating characterized by aggression, greed and social conflict. Humans – males particularly – began to carve up Planet Earth, fragmenting it eventually into arbitrary units that in time came to be known as *nation states*. And with the evolution of the nation state, warfare was normalized, inter-human aggression was exalted, and fierce competition infiltrated the human psyche, generating the capitalistic empire of the present time. In Taylor's own words (2005, 124):

> The Ego Explosion was the most momentous event in the history of the human race. The last 6,000 years of history can only be understood in terms of it. All the different kinds of social and psychic pathology – war, patriarchy, social stratification, materialism, the desire for status and power, sexual repression, environmental destruction, as well as the inner discontent and disharmony which afflict us – all these traits can be traced back to the intensified sense of ego which came into existence in the deserts of Saharasia 6,000 years ago.

In a word, *patriarchy* may be defined as the shadow side of the agricultural revolution. Historical and sociological text-books tend to laud all that was achieved in and through the agricultural breakthrough, but rarely are we told of the negative fallout, with diseases and illnesses unknown to humanity before that time, and social fallout that proved highly problematic for several ensuing millennia. (cf. Taylor 2005, 31, 39-40).

All forms of colonialism can be traced back to the colonization of land that transpired in the wake of the agricultural revolution, what Barker (2009) describes as the shift from foragers to farmers. The objectification and usurpation of the land was effectively pitching humans over against the organic planetary womb that had birthed and sustained humans for several millennia. With that painful serrating disruption, humans became a species in exile, estranged and alienated from the living God they had long known and served as the Great Spirit inhabiting the land itself. Not surprising, therefore, according to the Torah the restoration of the Jewish people could only be mediated through the land. Sadly, that noble aspiration itself became corrupted, as the organic soil came to be identified with the land of Israel, and its peoples exalted to an exclusively false status as the chosen people.

By the time of Jesus, the anthropocentric rhetoric had seriously undermined the priority of the land, its fertile inheritance, and its innate spiritual significance. It is noteworthy however that several of the parables critique the misappropriation of the land and the extensive exploitation of those who worked the soil. Several of the stories of demon-possession can also be interpreted as the infiltration of Roman oppression disempowering human initiative to the point of insanity due to the loss of their land and their inability to work the land in a truly organic way. Worthy of note at this juncture is Fanon's observation: "For a colonized people the most essential value, because the most concrete, is first and foremost the land: the land which will bring them bread and, above all, dignity." (Frantz Fanon 1963, 9).

Two other factors reinforce the culture of oppressive colonization, with misleading innocent names: *civilization* and *rationality*.

In virtually every field of learning, *civilization* is traced back to two features of the Neolithic period, c. 7,000-5,000 years ago: a) the evolution of written script in the ancient Sumerian culture, and b) the development of the first urban conglomerates in ancient Israel and elsewhere in the Middle East. With the evolution of the *polis* (city-state) it was easier for the leading patriarchs

64

to control and stratify human behavior. And by defining this new managerial philosophy as *civilization*, they were implicitly declaring as uncivilized everything that humans had achieved before that time. The convivial relationship with the land, what Taylor (2005, 112-113) calls "the primal empathy," and the deep organic spirituality that sustained people within the planetary web of life, all became demonized amid extensive dislocation, fragmentation and alienation. Not merely the people of Israel, but all humanity was driven into exile, not from God however, but from the organic web of life itself.

It was not merely the people who were driven into exile – so was the God humans had known and embraced for several centuries. Two long-cherished namings for this divine life-force – both highly controversial and effectively demonized in our patriarchally-infiltrated cultures – are those of the *Great Mother Goddess* (see Reid-Bowen 2007) and the *Great Spirit* (O'Murchu 2012). Both heavily emphasize the grounding of the sacred in the living earth itself. In both cases, humans did not worship a divine figurehead, rather they understood the divine life-force to be an innate cosmic reality which they were inspired to befriend and with which they were invited to co-create. Remnants of this ancient belief, which seems to have endured for at least 30,000 years, are still detectable in contemporary indigenous cultures.

Then came the rise of patriarchal domination, driven by fear and a compulsive need to control. Patriarchal males banished the Great Mother Goddess and suppressed the Great Spirit, and in their place they invented the Sky-God, a projection of their own insatiable desire for domination and control. This new deity was beyond the reach of all mortals, but could be partially accessed by divinely chosen males, and to the fore was *the king*, whose divinely-assigned role we will presently review.

The inflated male dominance now began to conjure up a second major deviation. Classical Greek philosophy, especially as developed by Plato and Aristotle, advocated that humans need to disassociate and separate themselves from the primitive enmeshment in nature – and all the perceived emotional attachments to the Great Mother Goddess. They were to do this by developing the capacity for *rational reason* – work it all out in the head, and disconnect from the body as much as possible. As the reader may know, Aristotle declared that men have the full potential for rationality, while women probably don't have such an endowment at all. And from that follows many centuries of misogynist oppression, fuelling colonial tyranny throughout much of the 2,000 years of Christendom and still bedeviling several contemporary strands of formal religion.

The colonial mindset which prevails today and is manifest in our politics, economics, social policy and religion, needs to be viewed within that long historical inheritance. There are four distinctive stages:

a) from the usurpation and fragmentation of the land (going back possibly 10,000 years),
b) to the progressive rise of patriarchal domination with the Sky-God in charge,
c) to the colonization of social stratification that came to be named as *civilization*,
d) to the prioritizing of reason and rationality over all other forms of human thought and discourse, ensnaring us in what Joerg Rieger (2007, 6) calls "our monodisciplinary slumbers."

A postcolonial critique requires us to name these developments, unmask their subtle but powerful influences, expose the infiltration of power and domination mediated through these influences, and finally wrestle with the residual baggage so that we can begin to transcend it and in time outgrow its debilitating and disempowering contagion. And we must not be dissuaded by the claim that for the Jewish people, ever faithful to the Torah, the sacredness of the land held high priority. That may have been the spiritual ideal to which many aspired; in practice, the imperial forces, both Jewish and Roman, viewed the land as a commodity for humans to use, and that more than anything else dictated the values that governed the use (and abuse) of land.

## Royal Intervention

Along this historical trajectory, another institutional construct came into being, one that has had enormous significance in the history of Christianity, namely *the evolution of kingship.* Many people assume that kings, and the governance of royal patronage, have been around for several millennia. Kingship also carries a cultural aura of immortality giving the impression that the power of the king is endowed with a kind of divine durability that transcends time and culture itself.

In terms of human history, and our evolutionary story of possibly 7,000,000 years (see O'Murchu 2009), kingship is a very recent visitor to the scene, born out of the cult of patriarchal domination, around 5,000 years ago. Two other institutional figures emerged around the same time: *the warrior on horseback* and *the male priest.* Prior to that time, clan and tribal rulers were the norm. It is widely assumed that they exercised power and control in a much more imposing and non-democratic way than kings would have done. *There is not a shred of evidence to substantiate this view – it is a classical patriarchal ploy of projecting onto our ancient ancestors the behaviors of the present time that we do not want to acknowledge or accept.* Although it is difficult to garner objective evidence (since much of it has been deliberately suppressed) the culture of Neolithic times suggests that clan and tribal leaderships embraced a more egalitarian and collaborative strategy.

Close affiliation with the land – particularly in pre-agricultural times - tends to encourage more cooperative and relational modes of human behavior.

With the evolution of kingship, human and earthly culture began to change dramatically. The patriarchal will to power becomes progressively disconnected from the convivial relationship with the land – and with the living Spirit who was perceived to be the source and sustainer of all life in creation. God is projected to an imperial throne above the sky, and humans are labeled as fickle and misguided. Consequently, the royal patriarch above the sky has to keep intervening to set things right. The primary construct for such intervention is that of the earthly king, who very quickly becomes divine as well – we see this illustrated overtly in the status attributed to Roman emperors. Around the same time, the priest evolves as a mediator between humans and the ruling God – but in this early dispensation (as evidenced in the Hebrew Scriptures) everything the priest does is dictated and controlled by the king.

We now have in place all the elements for widespread human and earthly alienation. The philosophy of divide-and-conquer is fragmenting not merely the land itself, it is actually destroying the long-term basis for human meaning and truth. And to rectify the mess the patriarchs themselves had created, they began to re-vision God as a kind of "Jim-will-fix-it" deity, who would intervene as deemed necessary. The Hebrew scripture (OT) is a litany of such interventions, directly and indirectly on the part of the ruling God. Most of those interventions are fantasized mental constructs of the patriarchs themselves, which the dominating wisdom duly sanctioned as revealed truth, in time to be declared the divine word of God. Self-inflation, cultural delusion, bizarre projection, and religious colonization infiltrate the Hebrew Scriptures from beginning to end.

On the contrary, the New Testament marks a radical departure from the regal monopoly, despite several attempts by both the (male) apostles and evangelists to maintain continuity and fidelity. As we shall see presently, those who created the oral narrative upon which the Gospels are based, and those who wrote the Gospels, exhibit ambivalence and ambiguity around the central sanctioned role of kingship. And when it comes to Jesus himself, there is such an unambiguous cleavage from imperial normalcy, it took not merely decades but centuries for Christianity to come to terms with that radical new dispensation named in Gospel lore as the *Kingdom of God*. Its dangerous memory will be unraveled in the next Chapter.

## Postcolonial Undercurrents of New Testament Writings

First however, I wish to scan briefly the major writings that constitute the New Testament. Consistently, we will encounter ambivalence and confusion. Clearly people of New Testament times – and particularly those who wrote and edited the writings that comprise the New Testament - detected what we now call a postcolonial dynamic. The normative culture of power and domination – sanctioned in the divinely mediated presence through the earthly king – infiltrated every aspect of life. Yet, a cultural shift was taking place, and with remarkable lucidity the life and ministry of Jesus illuminates the change that was in the air. The seismic shift is inherent to Jesus' initial allegiance to John the Baptist, followed by a choice for something much more radical, a shift several Christian commentators have failed to note. The rhythm of poetry best captivates the subversive move:

*Prepare Ye the Way!*

*The Baptist had them trembling with fear of things to come.*
*The ashes and the sackcloth,*

*The penance and the pain,*
*The fearful hand of judgement*
*What merit would they gain?*
*Apocalyptic vision – the frightening doom to come,*
*And the odds are stacked so heavy 'gainst those who would succumb.*

*Jesus joined the Baptist's rally, exploring future fate.*
*To seek his own vocation,*
*Excitement all around,*
*Awaiting the Messiah*
*The promised hopes abound.*
*But the people feel unworthy and are told they must repent*
*Lest they miss the golden moment of God's Messiah sent.*

*Jesus gazed upon the strategy and the Spirit led elsewhere.*
*He questioned the foundation*
*Of the fasting and the prayer*
*Envisioning alternatives*
*Of a strong prophetic flare.*
*Instead of disempowering those already colonized*
*He dreamt a new companionship with a dream to energize.*

*Jesus left aside the Baptist and chose another way.*
*The penance and the fasting,*
*The desert of the heart,*
*Instead let's dance in feasting*
*Set free and celebrate.*
*The powers were badly shaken, they could not comprehend*
*How people so transformed would throw convention to the wind.*

*They thought the other prophet was Elijah back once more.*
*The healing and the teaching,*
*Empowering liberty,*

*And the open common table,*
*Transgressing all decree.*
*While stories of empowerment, subversive to the core,*
*Their religion was in tatters with a future so unsure.*

*The attack upon the temple called the long awaited: halt!*
*The Baptist they beheaded,*
*For ethical repute;*
*But 'twas Roman crucifixion*
*Condemning Jesus mute.*
*Yet, companions for empowerment were already on the trail,*
*And the visionary from Magdala made sure it wouldn't fail.*

A new sense of power and empowerment was breaking through. Its postcolonial reverberations would be tried and tested but never muted. Its enduring challenge is felt afresh in the culture of the 21$^{st}$. century.

## The Letters of St. Paul

Paul's letters to the Thessalonians, Corinthians, Galatians, Romans, Philippians and Philemon are the earliest writings of the New Testament. For Paul, the clarion call that "Jesus is Lord" signals the invitation to a postcolonial critique. The word *Lord* occurs 717 times in the New Testament of which 275 references belong to the Pauline writings. Since this was a favorite title in Roman and Greek imperialism one wonders if Paul was contesting the prevailing power of Empire (which many scholars presume), or if Paul was implicitly colluding with it to validate his own power and the patriarchal values he seems – on occasion – to uphold and foster? In a word, to what extent is Paul, like many people at the time, ambivalent in his dealings with colonial and imperial power?

Before exploring this issue, we need to acknowledge the insightful research of Borg & Crossan (2009), suggesting that the Pauline writings fall into three categories, effectively portraying three Pauls rather than one. The first Paul seems to have been a radical visionary for inclusive empowerment and communal liberation, and we encounter him in the letters to Romans, I & 2 Corinthians, 1 Thessalonians, Galatians, Philippians and Philemon. The second Paul is a much more conservative character encouraging slaves to obey their masters and wives to be subject to their husbands – in the disputed letters of Ephesians, Colossians and 2 Thessalonians. The third is the reactionary Paul of 1 & 2 Timothy and Titus, tamed and co-opted by the values of the imperial culture. Having reviewed some of the leading theorists on the postcolonial Paul, I'll return to the question of who might be the authentic historical Paul.

Richard Horsley's postcolonial reflection on Paul is deemed to be one of the more authoritative statements on Paul's anticolonial stance (Horsley 1997; Horsley 1998). Contrary to the individualistic, depoliticized popularization of Paul, through Augustine and Luther, emphasizing personal righteousness and salvation, Paul's foundational mission was much more social and political in nature:

> Paul understood the project in which he was engaged as the founding or building of an alternative society. . . . His own Gospel of an alternative history disrupted and replaced the Roman imperial narrative but did that through direct interaction with the bold borrowing from the dominant culture. He entered and mixed with the discourse of the dominant Western metropolitan culture in order to transform it. (Horsley 1998, 165)

72

In Paul's view, patronage networks were already softening the power of the Empire towards wider social engagement and empowerment. Paul, therefore, opted for a program of alternative small communities, borrowing from the *ekklesia* model of secular government at the time. Through these alternative communities Paul began to mold an different meta-history in resistance to Roman domination, promoting new structures to facilitate personal liberation, along with social and political transformation. Horsley summarizes the attempt in these words: "How seriously Paul took his counter-imperial Gospel, of the counter-imperial Savior, and the counter-imperial government, is indicated in his almost excessive building of 'assemblies' and his instructions to them in their relations with the world." (Horsley 1998, 69).

Other scholars adopt a less complementary view of Paul, such as Joseph Marchal who writes:

> Paul is not just repeating imperial images in his letters; he is also mimicking imperial-style power arrangements in an effort to consolidate his own authority. . . . The arrangements are neither leveling nor inclusive, but hierarchical and exclusive. . . . In the end, even if one can manage to argue that all this time Paul is working to overthrow the exploitative Roman Empire, it becomes hard to deny how easily adaptable Paul's rhetorical methods are to an imperial agenda. (Marchal 2007, 57).

Christopher D. Stanley (2011) provides a comprehensive overview of Paul's immersion in a colonized culture and how it influenced his perceptions and judgments. According to the *Acts of the Apostles*, Luke presents Paul as one who courted the good favor of Rome and its political leadership, to a final point where Paul, the prisoner, enjoys a strange degree of mobility and freedom from within the site of his captivity. This is probably an inflated Lukan account. Paul certainly tried to engage the powers of Rome and win their good favor to support his ministry of evangelization, but in the process borrowed so much from the imperial culture that he may stand accused of more collusion (mimicry) than mutual collaboration.

The picture is further complicated by the notion of the three Paul's, explored by Borg & Crossan (2009), an insightful reconstruction that none of the contributors to Christopher Stanley's monograph seem to employ. Clearly the Paul of the Pastoral Epistles is significantly more patriarchal and 'colonial' than in the letters assigned to what Borg and Crossan call the first Paul. Despite an already formidable corpus of research on Paul's postcolonial status, it looks likely a great deal has yet to be investigated.

From the mid-twentieth century onward, scholars embarked on the *new perspective* on our understanding of the Pauline heritage. In an attempt to broaden the inherited Protestant emphasis on law, justification and good works, with a distinctive focus on individual salvation, scholars shifted more towards ecclesial, social and even political understandings of Paul's teachings and his evangelical vision. (For a valuable summary, see webpage: http://www.thepaulpage.com/a-summary-of-the-new-perspective-on-paul/). Among other things, scholars wanted to rehabilitate Paul the Jew, whose primary goal, it seems, was to reform Judaism and not create a new religion (Christianity).

The new perspective endeavours to honour a complexity in Pauline thought that more conventional scholarship has either ignored or bypassed. Firstly, are the complexities of Paul the human being, the Jew, the zealous evangelizer, but also the person with a strong social conscience, the catalyst for alternative community formation, and the fierce critic (it would seem) of imperial domination. Paul was certainly concerned about individual spiritual integrity, but most often – it now appears – within a structural and communal context that also needed to be subject to the spiritual transformation he pursued so zealously.

Finally, there are many scribal renditions of Paul's words, deeds and achievements that need to be reviewed within the journalistic strategies and standards of the time. Increasingly, scholars are critical of Luke's inflated portrayal of Paul in the *Acts of the Apostles*, wherein many details are not congruent with what are considered to be Paul's own authentic writings. We also need to remember that in early Christian times, the attribution of a letter to a particular individual – in this case Paul – does not necessarily mean that the person in question is the actual author of that piece of writing. Hence the claim by Borg & Crossan that most of the Pauline writings are not first-hand material of the man himself, and that some (eg., the Pastoral Epistles) may contain material quite alien to the more authentic Paul.

Postcolonial critique seeks to expose and dismantle the aberrations of imperial power, most of all as embodied in texts that have impacted on the exercise of power in cultural and religious settings. The writings of St. Paul have been extensively influential, and have been frequently used to promote powerful orthodoxy in social, political and religious spheres. To unearth the more authentic Paul, the critic of imperial domination, and at times its victim, is a work in progress that deserves all the attention and discernment that can be brought to the undertaking.

## The Four Gospels

a) *Mark*: Tat-siong Benny Liew, currently *Professor of New Testament at the College of the Holy Cross in Worcester, Massachusetts*, describes Mark's Gospel as a colonial mimetic discourse representing tyranny, boundary and might, claiming that Mark mimics Roman imperial ideology even in his attempt to challenge it (Liew

1999a). Mark reproduces the authority of the Roman Empire in a Jesus who appears to be running around the countryside ordering people like a tyrant. Thus Mark sets up a new insider-outsider binarism wherein those who respond favorably to Jesus, the authoritative interpreter and fulfillment of God's will, are 'in,' and those who do not are 'out.' Mark's Jesus may have sought alternatives to Jewish-Roman power, but according to Liew, the tyrannical, exclusionary and coercive politics goes on. Using colonial mimicry, Mark internalized the imperialist ideology of the colonizers by (1) attributing absolute authority to Jesus, (2) preserving the same insider/outsider binarism, and (3) its understanding of the nature of 'legitimate' authority (Liew 1999b: 13).

Other scholars such as Simon Samuel (2007), while acknowledging postcolonial ambivalence in Mark's Gospel, deem Liew's critique to be too harsh and heavy-handed. Richard Horsley (2003) claims that the authentic Mark is consistently anti-imperial, a stance not upheld by subsequent redactors: "Established Christianity co-opted Mark, and established Western Biblical studies have effectively kept Mark's narrative of a submerged people's history of renewal from re-emerging (Horsley 2003, 161). Samuel (2007) argues that Mark's Jesus is the subject of a complex colonial/postcolonial narrative, simultaneously accommodating and disrupting the dominant culture. Mark's discourse tries to negotiate that interstitial space between Roman imperial and authoritative Jewish discourses by constructing a portrait of Jesus that is both affiliative and disruptive to the Jewish tradition from which it arises, and the Roman domination it seeks to displace.

b) *Matthew*: Warren Carter, currently Professor of New Testament at Brite Divinity School in Forth Worth, Texas, has authored an intensive study on *Matthew and Empire* (Carter 2001), generally regarded by scholars as one of the more authoritative works on this topic. Carter claims that *Matthew's Gospel* both contests and resists the Roman Empire's claims to sovereignty over the world. It sustains an alternative community of disciples of Jesus in anticipation of the coming triumph of God's Empire over all things, including the destruction of Rome's Empire. That is to say, the Gospel resists Rome with a social challenge by offering a vastly different vision and experience of human community, and with a theological challenge in asserting that the world belongs to God not to Rome, that God's purposes run through Israel and Jesus, not via Rome.

Matthew's Gospel opens with a long genealogy tracing Jesus to ancient Jewish sources, thus proffering a counterclaim to the imperial divinity invoked in Roman supremacy. Carter first describes the nature of Roman imperialism, particularly as it would have existed in Syrian Antioch, where many scholars think Matthew's Gospel was written. Besides an unimaginable life of overcrowded city streets, crumbling tenements, filth, disease, and endless threats of plague, drought, and war, conquered peoples in the ancient world could not avoid the ubiquitous presence of thousands of Roman soldiers for whose support they were heavily taxed. The Jewish people would have been constantly reminded of their inferiority and subjection to the Romans, especially since they had been so devastated by the Roman victory over their people in the brutal Jewish-Roman war which lasted form 66-73 CE.

Matthew's Gospel is a response to this exclusivist, fragmented, and uncaring climate. The message of Jesus is "inclusive, egalitarian, merciful"(Carter 2001, 51). Carter examines several texts that demonstrate how the gospel resists Roman imperialism and lifts up an alternative community of disciples who look forward to the full establishment of God's reign, rather than Rome's domination.

Yet throughout his book, Carter notes a major irony characterizing Matthew's Gospel. In spite of presenting an egalitarian community as a challenge to Rome's imperialism, Matthew imitates the imperial worldview as much as he resists it. Judgment is a strong theme in Matthew, and God's violent revenge, not reconciliation, is promised upon those who have operated outside God's Empire. Moreover, the Great Commission of Matthew 28:18-20 uses imperialist assumptions in "making disciples of all nations."

c) *Luke-Acts*: Since Luke is considered to be the author of both his named Gospel of Luke and the Acts of the Apostles I combine the two works in this reflection. Both of Luke's books begin with an auspicious greeting to an exalted patron: "Theophilus, his excellency" (Lk.1:1-4; Acts 1:1). It looks like Luke is trying to reach members of the elite, ruling class. It is generally believed that Luke wrote his Gospel between 80-85 CE during a time of immense conflict between Christianity and the Roman Empire. Luke's gospel can be seen as an ideological tool to reach out, and make peace with the Romans (176). Thus writes Richard A. Horsley (2008, 181): "The book of Acts, on the surface of the text at least, appears to have made serious accommodations to the Roman Empire, to the point of blaming 'the Jews' for its troubles in order to appear less threatening to the Empire. Its author, however, still sees the wider movement of Christ believers as spreading steadily across the Empire as an alternative social order, however compromised."

Virginia Burrows (in Segovia and Sugirtharajah 2009, 142) claims (along with other scholars cited) that Luke's writings are best understood as addressed to the philanthropic rich. His many allusions to the poor tend to be couched in paternalistic language. Similarly, he frequently names women, but tends to depict them in a patronizing way, casting them in co-dependent roles. This is particularly striking in his treatment of Martha and Mary, sisters co-equal in ministry (in all probability) dualistically split into a passively over-spiritualized Mary, and a negatively portrayed active Martha.

Interestingly, I have not encountered any commentator who has detected the postcolonial disaster of Luke's Pentecostal narrative. In Acts 2:1-11, Luke narrates a special gathering of the reconstituted twelve (apostles) in the upper room in which they receive the commissioning empowerment of the Holy Spirit to go forth to preach and teach. There is no trace of the foundational layer of Christian discipleship led by Mary Magdalene and several women (and presumably some men also). It looks like Luke has brutally obliterated the original disciples – despite a subtle reference in Acts 1:14 - in order to lay a solid apostolic foundation for his two great heroes, namely Peter and Paul. This must surely be one of the most oppressive colonial deviations in the entire New Testament; I will return to the subject in later chapters.

d) *John's Gospel:* This is a highly symbolic treatise in which little or nothing can be taken literally. It is written as a theological reflection on the life and ministry of Jesus, with limited attention to historical fact. Jesus is portrayed as the only authentic incarnation of God's fatherly care for humanity, a designation perfectly fulfilled by the historical Jesus in his unmitigated allegiance to the Father, even to the point of death. Throughout John's Gospel, Jesus is portrayed as the new Moses, fulfilling the divine prerogative of the ancient God described as "I am who am." Jesus, too, asserts his designated oneness with this father-God in the 'I am' statements (e.g., 6:48, 8:12, 11:25), the subject of several commentaries.

At its face value, the portrayal of Jesus is that of a self-assured, messianic, powerful, divine figurehead before whom all other creatures must bow in submission. For the Botswanan postcolonial scholar, Musa W. Dube, such a depiction is unambiguously of colonial intent: "I therefore hold that the Johannine approach of exalting Jesus to divine status, above all Jewish figures, and above all other cultural figures of the world, is a colonizing ideology . . . that claims power over all other places and peoples of the earth." (Dube in Sugirtharajah 1998,131-132).

The Jesus who seems to attribute to himself a king-like status (Jn.18:36), is clearly a different divine representative from the counter-cultural Jesus of the Synoptic Gospels. But is this king-like construct symbolic rather than literal, and if so how do we discern the deeper meaning? Within the symbolism is there a subversive attempt at exposing the false domination of Roman and Jewish imperialism? And if so, might the author of John's gospel also stand accused of colonial mimicry? Responding to such questions, Stephen D. Moore (2006, 50) describes John's Gospel as the most – and the least – political of the canonical Gospels. "For ultimately," Moore writes, "the Johannine resistance to Roman colonization might be said to be an alternative program of colonization yet more ambitious than the Roman: the annexation of the world by non-military means." (Moore 2006, 70).

Fernando Segovia (in Segovia & Sugirtharajah 2009, 156-193) endorses this critique claiming that John's Gospel presents a bipolar conflicted reality: the other-world and this-world, with the latter proclaimed as more enduring and authentic. The clash of these worlds corresponds to a rival system of power, portraying an all-powerful God upon whom all creatures are passively and helplessly dependent. The ensuing conflict culminates in the death and Resurrection of Jesus in which, Segovia argues, a postcolonial program is unfolded, resulting in the victory of the kingdom of God, represented by Jesus and his followers, over the kingdom of Satan, represented by Jewish and Roman authorities. In conclusion, Segovia problematizes the Gospel's oppositional space, describing it as a "highly unstable anti-imperial colonial imperialism" that borrows "too much from its target for its own good." (ibid, 192).

We encounter ambiguity in all four Gospels, a topic requiring ongoing discernment and attention in the hope that eventually Christians - and others - can outgrow the ambivalence which has long characterized the inheritance of our faith. I conclude this brief overview of Gospel ambiguity with this poetic synthesis:

*The Gospel's Colonial Echoes*

*Liberty to captives and freedom to the poor,*
*Echoes for a breakthrough, to hope it would endure.*
*Countering the forces the empire values most,*
*With internalized oppression like an archetypal ghost.*
*The portrayal is oft ambiguous, unsure where Jesus stands*
*Or is it the Evangelists who undermine his plans?*
*Did Jesus really compromise a woman to a dog*
*Or is that the Gospel writer in a patriarchal fog?*
*Did Jesus give endorsement that Israel should be first*
*Thus relegating all the rest, a strange oppressive twist?*
*In either case we evidence colonial veneer*
*Disrupting the empowerment God's New Reign did declare.*
*The Lukan Jesus mingles much time among the rich*
*And demands the poor converting submit to what he preach.*
*The inner core consulting is Peter, James and John;*
*One wonders if the Magdalene was largely left anon!*
*We need to question Holy Writ for justice to procure.*
*Exposing the distortions oft making power secure.*
*Even Jesus must be rescued from the patriarchal trance.*
*As companions for empowerment prophetic'ly advance.*

## The Book of Revelation

The Book of Revelation is a polemic against the imperial cult, and a warning to the early Christians not to engage with it. The imagery shows that good triumphs over evil, that faithfulness will be rewarded and justice will be done. The author develops a complex symbolic plot highlighting the defeat of evil and the establishment of a New Jerusalem. The hero, or protagonist, is Jesus. Satan is the antagonist, the ultimate adversary.

Stephen D. Moore (in Segovia & Sugirtharajah 2009, 436ff) provides a fine overview of the many recent commentaries adopting a postcolonial critique of Revelation. The whore of Babylon is clearly the Roman Empire, perhaps with the persecutions of Nero as a specific focus, or the destruction of the temple c.70 CE. The Beast (Satan) is contrasted with the Lamb (Jesus). Some commentators suggest that the seven seals serve as a symbolic counterpart for the seven hills of Rome.

While Revelation provides a blistering critique on the evils of empire, the proposed counter-culture seems to adopt several of the same violently destructive strategies to bring about the desired resolution. Moore (ibid, 446) captivates the deep ambivalence when he writes:

> The phenomenon of mimicry is endemic to Revelation. The book's representation of Roman imperial order is essentially parodic, and parody is a species of mimicry: it mimics in order to mock. . . Revelation's attempted sleight of hand ensnares it in a debilitating contradiction. Christians are enjoined to mimic Jesus, who in turn mimics his Father, who, in effect mimics the Roman emperor, who himself (at least as represented in the imperial cult) is a mimetic composite of assorted royal and divine stereotypes. In Revelation, Christian authority inheres in imitation, . . . if the Roman imperial order is the ultimate object of imitation in Revelation, then, in accordance with the book's own implicit logic, it remains the ultimate authority, despite the book's explicit attempts to unseat it.

## Constantine's Shadow

Although difficult to establish with verifiable evidence, the early Christians seem to have detected the new anti-imperial shift, and as Candida Moss (2013, 163ff.) points out, Christians as a religious group, were unique in contesting the values and powers of the Empire. Up to and until the early fourth century when things changed dramatically as new colonial forces came to the fore. Constantine was the primary catalyst, with some vestiges of earlier influence. For Constantine, Jesus was the all powerful ruler (the *Pantocrator*), who con-validated every form of raw power so important for Constantine's dominance and control. Long after Constantine had faded from history, however, his addictive lure to power continued to flourish in the Christian Church. It is all too obvious in linear Church authority, exhibited in the Catholic papacy and in the leading institutional structures of several Christian institutions.[5]

And in every case, it is upheld in the name of Gospel wisdom. But what wisdom? Or, more accurately, whose wisdom? We are told that the Gospels are embedded in divine revelation. They portray the fullness of God's truth for all time. It is however a truth circumscribed by several caveats that rarely have been named or critiqued.

The inspiration of scripture (revelation) became a hotly debated issue in the second and third centuries of the Christian era. Invoking a postcolonial cipher, Pui-lan Kwok (1995), draws our attention to the fluidity and diversity that prevailed in the earliest strands of Christian theology and particularly in Christology itself. In 1990, the British scholar, James G. D. Dunn had already published a seminal work highlighting the vastly diverse understandings that characterize all aspects of the New Testament, including Christology (Dunn 1990). With the emergence of Constantine and the formal adoption of Christianity as the Roman state religion ". . .such open-ended and fluid Christology became a threat to the expanding Roman Empire, when imperial unity required some kind of doctrinal conformity. . . . The Canon (of Scripture) became necessary in the politics of truth to demarcate orthodoxy and heresy, and to consolidate power by the Church hierarchy" (Kwok 1995, 172, 8).

There are several features in the doctrinal development of early Christianity that postcolonalists wish us to confront:

1. All the key participants were European males, of elite learned status. Women had no say whatever; in other words half of God's human creatures were barred from the process. The poor and marginalized – the bulk of society - were not asked for their wisdom. And, of course, nobody would have considered if the non-human world might have something to contribute to our understanding of God's revelation.

2. Why was access to God considered to be so elitist and exclusive? Partly, because of the influence of Greek culture at the time. Rational debate was the way to arrive at truth, and only those endowed with the power of reason – namely men - could participate. And they arrived at the truth depending on their power to argue their case. So where does discernment come into play – if at all?

3. The Church debates – in Council or otherwise – were meant to be about the things of God, and how the Holy One relates to life. In several cases, it was political power that was driving the process, and political expediency dictated the outcome. St. Augustine's just war theory largely ignores Gospel non-violence, and the passive resistance that characterized early Christian times. The theory was drawn up to allow – and justify – the Church itself to go to war.

4. The meaning of *revelation* (revealed truth) is for humans only. It is narrowly anthropocentric. Creation is rarely referred to. The sacredness of the land – God's great gift to the people in the O.T. covenant – seems to have faded into oblivion. Today, we understand God's primary revelation to be the created universe itself, thus begetting a huge hermeneutical chasm between contemporary wisdom and early Christian doctrine.[6]

"Get back to the Gospels" is a modern slogan echoed among those who feel we have betrayed our foundational Christian wisdom, or seriously lost our way as a Christian people. The reversion, however, is often naive and simplistic. Gospel wisdom is increasingly seen to be complex, profound, and requiring an interdisciplinary mode of engagement to access the deeper truth. In this process – embraced by adult-seekers in our time – it is not merely about 'going back'. It is much more about *moving forward* – as evolution always does – using the Gospels as a resource upon which we build and reconstruct. As I shall indicate in subsequent chapters of this book, the Gospel Jesus is very much a *forward-looking* visionary strategy imbued with a radically empowering dynamic that has eluded scholars - and churches – for several centuries.

Before we get to Jesus, however, there is a good deal of clutter to clear away – as postcolonial studies seek to do. To the fore is the royal baggage of kingly imperialism, elucidated in the Gospels under the rubric of the Kingdom of God. We have briefly encountered its extensive impact, requiring a more penetrating analysis outlined in the next Chapter.

## Concluding Resume

The reflections of this Chapter resemble the synthesis furnished by Ralph Broadbent (in Liew 2009, 301), who proposes the following challenges to religious and biblical fundamentalism, arising from the unique insights of postcolonialism:

- We need a multi-faith and multicultural perspective, refusing to allow one particular religious tradition the final word.
- Postcolonialism openly challenges religious power by pointing to the parallels between the exercise of religious authority and imperial power.
- Authoritative religious texts are problematized as violent and intolerant propaganda and their authority questioned.
- Other texts, both religious and secular, are seen as conveying truth.
- Suppressed dissenting voices are recovered.
- Christianity is shown to be influenced by non-Christian faiths and is thereby relativized.
- The message of the Christian faith, despite having some anti-imperial aspects, is shown to be a mirror reflection of the violent Roman Empire.
- The figure of Jesus is converted into an imperial figure, who will return in power and glory – by implication, bringing death and vengeance.

Christian spirituality invites the devotee to take on the mind of Christ, and thus be molded more fully in the image and likeness of God. Postcolonialism brings to our attention the cultural filters and historical ingredients that have colored – and continue to influence – our inherited faith. There is no such thing as an objective divine revelation – all wisdom, divine, and otherwise is mediated, not merely through the limitations of human learning, but more significantly by all that impacts upon our cultural conditioning. Because patriarchal power has been heavily sanctioned, and unrelentingly indoctrinated over several millennia, then it is ingrained in several aspects of our lives, at personal and systemic levels. It will not easily be undone!

Only an extensive shift in consciousness will bring about its demise. Several movements of the late 20th century – liberation, feminist, ecological, communitarian, quantum physics - awoke new understandings and expanded levels of comprehension. Despite 'business as usual' in several fields - especially in politics, economics, social policy and religion – an extended awareness that every whole is greater than the sum of its parts, augments an awakening that cannot be reversed and will in time forge open new horizons of vision and fresh possibility.

The postcolonial critique, more than any other contemporary movement, is eminently poised to activate this new transformation. By undermining one of the most resilient of all resistances – the patriarchal will to power – it paves the way for that liberating breakthrough which several movements of the late 20th century anticipated but were unable to deliver in an enduring way. This time the critique is more penetrating, the emerging insights more empowering and encouraging, and the commitment necessary for an enduring breakthrough is more solidly grounded. There is good reason to be optimistically hopeful.

# Chapter 5:
## *Kingship Colonizes the Gospels*

*The most hybridized concept of the Christian tradition is that of Jesus/Christ. The space between Jesus and Christ is unsettling and fluid, resisting easy categorization and closure. . . . The richness and vibrancy of the Christian community is diminished whenever the space between Jesus and Christ is fixed.*

Kwok Pui-Lan

*Throughout its history, Christology has been employed both in support and in critique of empire, and often there is only a thin line between the two.*

Joerg Rieger.

In August 2010, Amphon Tangnoppakul, a Thai truck driver, was arrested for sending insulting text messages about a member of the Thai royal family. Despite claiming that he did not even know how to send text messages, he was convicted and sentenced to a 20 year prison term in November 2011, and died in prison (of mouth cancer) in May 2012. To those seeking the abolition of such draconian laws, Amphon came to be known as Uncle SMS.

Amphon was charged and imprisoned not solely because of his derogatory remarks about a member of the royal household, but because he 'blasphemed' against God himself. To many people this may seem a ridiculous piece of outdated bureaucracy, but in fact it serves as a timely reminder of the postcolonial left-over from several centuries past whereby kingly rule is deemed to be synonymous with divine governance. We are describing a belief known as *the divine right of kings*! In broad strokes the story goes like this.

God is a King, who rules from the heights of heaven. Heaven is above; the earth and all it contains is beneath. The divine rulership is mediated through the earthly king. Only the king can authoritatively represent God's rule on earth. Therefore the king is effectively divine, and should be honored and respected as a divine figurehead.

Historically, it is difficult to trace the precise origins of this development. It dominated ancient Chinese political and social life. The ruling God(s) of Hinduism – the oldest formal religion known to us – embodies royal dignity and commands a quality of allegiance identical to political kingship. The impact on Christianity tends to be traced from the Assyrians, thereafter, to the Medes, the Persians, the Macedonians, the Jews and down to the Romans who invaded the Palestine in 63 BCE.

## The Anthropocentric Underlay

The anthropocentric subtleties deserve closer scrutiny, and often escape the discernment of rigorous scholarship. On earth, human beings are deemed to be the superior life-form, with everything else considered to be for human use and benefit. This is stated explicitly in Gen.1:26-28. While several scholars claim that the Hebrew nuances do not support such overt human control and manipulation, the text has been extensively used to justify the human urge to divide and conquer.

Not merely is the human in charge and in control, but is also construed as the one who stands over against, and apart from, the natural world. In Chapter Four above, I have already reviewed the emergence of civilization in the fourth and fifth centuries before the Christian era. Civilized humans were required to extricate themselves from their enmeshment in the natural world. They were to stand apart in the unique, imperial, divinely-mandated status of being the creatures closest to God, enthroned in the trans-earthly heavenly realm.

And these humans chosen to be God's primary representatives on earth had to be *male*. According, to Aristotle, females are misbegotten males, and consequently are incapable of truly representing divine power. Again, it is difficult to trace earlier evidence for this extreme misogyny, but undoubtedly it prevailed long before Aristotle gave it such virulent affirmation.

Combining all the above factors, we can glean the kind of discernment that would have been adopted – both by rulers and rank-and-file – at the beginning of the Christian era, when several contenders were claiming to be messianic ambassadors from God. It was a millennial epoch. Change was in the air. God was expected to make a new breakthrough (variously understood) and in the Jewish world, there was no shortage of contenders for the honorific role of restoring the ancient kingdom of King David.

One question guided the search to differentiate the authentic from the fraudulent: "Is there royal blood in the background?" If the response is negative, then you simply ignore and forget such contenders. If the response suggests that some distant relatives belonged to one or other royal lineage, then one would need to check for a direct line of descent; nothing short of a direct line is adequate.

The Gospels of Matthew (1:1-17) and Luke (3:23-38) provide the direct line of descent, back to King David in the case of Matthew, back to Abraham in the case of Luke. To the best of my knowledge, there is not a shred of evidence for the veracity of either genealogy. We are dealing with a literary construct, which the writers felt obliged to include to make their claims credible.

Such was the influence of divine royal imperialism at the time of the historical Jesus.

Early Christianity quite unambiguously embraces and endorses the divine royal dispensation. Jesus was envisaged as the one who would restore the throne of David (a theme re-echoed in the Advent Christian liturgy even in our own time), the one the apostles sought to re-enthrone as their divine king on earth, and were extremely baffled when Jesus did not concede to their wishes. The one who, according to the four evangelists, underwent formal trials before his death – as if he were a king - when in fact he was being crucified as a subversive! Subversives rarely had the benefit of any trial, royal or otherwise.

## From Greek to Aramaic

Throughout the Gospels, according to the English rendering of the Greek, Jesus spoke frequently of the *Kingdom of God*. Scholars of the 20th century moved toward a strong consensus that the notion of the Kingdom of God, more than anything else, clarifies for us how Jesus envisaged his mission on earth, and how he wanted humans to embrace that mission. Two thousand years later, it is impossible to establish how the early disciples heard this statement – and its elaborate explanation in several parables. Did they hear the historical Jesus endorsing the culture of divinely inspired kingship, or did they detect a deeply subversive counterculture, turning kingship, and all the royal values, on its head?

We know that power is always at work in our human and divine contexts, even within religion itself. And in so far as the Gospels encapsulate the vision of our faith as a Christian people, we need to confront the power-dynamics that prevailed – then and now – in how we appropriate and live our faith. Much more demanding is the task of identifying what belongs to the postcolonial baggage, and what belongs authentically to the vision and mission of the historical Jesus.

Scripture scholars have been addressing these questions, particularly throughout the 19th and 20th centuries. The academic pursuit took on an added momentum after the Second World War when scholars (particularly in Europe) began to look afresh at the notion of the *Kingdom of God*. Having first identified the various allusions to the Kingdom as central to the meaning of the Gospel message – considered to be the *primary* material to understand the message of Jesus – they then tried to unravel the complex and diverse set of meanings embodied in the concept itself. That exploration continues till the present time.

In the final decades of the 20th century, some scholars began to address the significance of what came to be known as the *Jewish Jesus* (e.g., Geza Vermes, E.P. Sanders), including cultural artifacts (e.g., language) belonging to his indigenous culture. While the Gospels are written in Greek, the oral message they embody would have been delivered in Aramaic, Jesus' indigenous Palestinian language. As a spoken language, the meaning conveyed by the Aramaic is determined by the quality of sound, whereas Greek as a written language tends to be judged by what we see on a page. The parables, the Sermon on the Mount, and the several sayings attributed to Jesus would most likely have been delivered in some form of ancient Aramaic, and the people would have heard the words with all the nuances accompanying the indigenous oral tradition.

Trying to retrieve this ancient material is notoriously difficult, since Aramaic was a spoken language only (Hebrew being one written equivalent), and therefore the words spoken became part of a narrative repeated many times in the oral tradition with all the embellishments that accompany the art of story-telling. Moreover, since Greek – the language in which the Gospels were written – was deemed to be the culturally superior language of the day, the medium to capture and communicate significant truth, many scholars are reluctant to tamper with the Greek text, all the more so when it is declared to be the revealed Word of God. Once again, postcolonial viewers look askance, and suspect that this is another example of a totalizing device in which the subaltern voice (the indigenous wisdom) becomes displaced by that which was granted exalted status (namely the emerging Greek culture).

Throughout the land of Israel, in the time of Jesus, Greek had become the leading lingo of economics, politics and learning. It was the language in which business and education was transacted. The evangelists chose to publish the Gospels in Greek in the sure hope that they would compete with all other forms of official knowledge that prevailed in the culture of the day. And in due course they were validated when the Roman Emperor Constantine legalized the adoption of the Christian faith early in the fourth century, paving the way for the Emperor Theodosius to declare Christianity as the official religion of the Empire in 380CE. In the process of such accommodation, however, did we lose something quite precious, from the earlier indigenous culture? More significantly, did Constantine's imperial religion, which dominated all the Christian churches well into the 20th century, seriously undermine the prophetic egalitarianism originally proclaimed by Jesus?

As yet, a mere handful of scholars are addressing this huge cultural and contextual challenge; American researcher, Orville Boyd Jenkins, provides a comprehensive overview.[7] Aramaic and Greek seem to be quite different languages, embracing quite diverse worldviews. Greek being the intellectually approved language of the day, with the prospect of forwarding progress and development at every level of life, largely abandoned the more indigenous, earth-centered and more collaborative spirit of the Aramaic. Greek supported the literature of kingship; in all probability, ancient Aramaic did not.

In an earlier work (O'Murchu 2012), I run with the popularized notion that an Aramaic rendering of the Kingdom of God would translate into something akin to the *Companionship of Empowerment*. This marks a clear departure from the culture of imperial kingship. Here Jesus is breaking clean from his inherited Jewish wisdom and purporting a radically different understanding of God and the divine desire for God's reign on earth. *Empowerment*, rather than power-over, becomes the core value, and the dynamics of *mutuality and community-building* (companionship) displace the unilateral control from the top down.

How did the people respond, the rank-and-file seeking liberation and hope beyond the colonial oppression of Roman imperialism and the often-collusive support of the Jewish priestly classes? And how would the powers-that-be, convinced of their divine right to dominate and control, have responded. The South African scholar, Albert Nolan (1976, 122) captivates the mood in these provocative words:

> It would have been impossible for the people of Jesus' time to have thought of him as an eminently religious man who steered clear of political action. They would have seen him as a blasphemously irreligious man who under the cloak of religion was undermining all the values upon which religion, politics, economics and society were based. He was a dangerous and subtly subversive revolutionary.

## Subversive shift from power to empowerment

Many years ago, as a young student training for priesthood, I attended a preached retreat. The opening reflection was based on St. Paul's letter to the Philippians (2:5-11), a text frequently used (I was told) in the opening session of week-long retreats. The preacher kept the focus on the phrase: "Have that mind in you which was also in Christ Jesus" and went on to explain in great deal what he understood the mind of Christ to be about. Devoid of all sense of a postcolonial critique, neither I nor any other participant challenged his interpretation. In fact it would be several more years before the dangerous and misleading indoctrination would become apparent to any of us.

The preacher emphasized that the mind of Christ involved total abandonment to God our father (at great length, he cited John's Gospel to show how Jesus did this), unquestioned obedience – even to the point of death, submission, humility, suffering for its own sake, and a willingness to be perceived as worthless. Jesus was totally in the hands of God his father, for the father to do with him as he wished. As Christians, we, too, should embrace this humble abandonment and become totally obedient to God's representatives on earth, namely, the Pope, Bishops, Superiors, etc. For the preacher, this was the mind of Christ, and he garnered extensive evidence from the New Testament to convince us of the veracity of his message.

Indeed, St. Anselm's theory of Atonement – as popularly understood - sounds quite similar: the God-man who condescends to being obedient like a child and subservient to the whim and fancy of his punitive father. It is a co-dependent set of values that have been espoused by Christianity over many centuries. Today, the same tendency prevails more overtly in Islam than in the other major world religions.

If we begin our discernment of Christian faith – in the spirit and mind of the Gospels - then one wonders how could we ever have ended up with such a convoluted interpretation. *"Seek first the Kingdom of God and his justice . . ."* seems an unambiguously clear guideline. It is the primary task of Christian belief, and a foundational guide to discerning the mind of Christ. Translating that vision in terms of the *Companionship of Empowerment*, it becomes all too obvious that Christian discipleship has nothing to do with passive obedience and humiliating victim-hood. To the contrary, we cannot hope to mediate for others the empowering liberation of the Gospels until firstly we internalize the experience of self-empowerment.

This is merely another rendition of the great commandment: *love God and love the neighbor,* and the extent to which we show genuine love for the God we cannot see depends on how genuinely we love the neighbor we do see. However, the language of love can easily be domesticated, and the meaning of love can all too quickly be trivialized. Gospel love, in terms of the Companionship of Empowerment, is what might best be described as *tough love,* love wedded strongly with justice and liberation from all oppression. This is the love mediated in the Gospels through the subversive stories of the parables, the transformative healing rendered through the miracles, and the subversive fidelity that defies even death itself.

Before looking more closely at each of these three dimensions - parables, miracles, subversive fidelity - a word of clarification is necessary on the challenge of Christian subversiveness. It is often associated with prophetic witness, with the incisive critique of dominant power, and the provocative imagination that proffers alternatives to the royal consciousness (more in Brueggemann 1978; 1984). In the life of the historical Jesus it culminates in *a total renunciation* of kingship and all the imperial values upon which it flourished. This is vividly illustrated in Jesus' last journey into Jerusalem when he allowed the disciples to regard him as a king (something he always abhorred), but chose to ride on a donkey. This is by far the most subversive of all the parables although I don't know of any scripture scholar who describes the story as a parable.

Kings always rode on horses. Despite some examples in the Hebrew Scriptures of kings riding donkeys, the horse is typically considered to be the royal beast, also being the animal best suited for the violent warrior, the king's right-hand resource for the implementation of imperial power. The donkey was the beast of burden for the rural people of Galilee, employed daily for a range of domestic chores. One wonders if the disciples - so indoctrinated in divine kingly ideology – got any of the highly subversive symbolism? The *pyramid* of divinely sanctioned kingship had been collapsed into the *circle* of the ordinary folk, accompanying their donkeys in a variety of daily tasks. The royal dispensation had been dismantled into the communal empowerment arising from the ground up. And undoubtedly, some - witnessing the scene - would recall Zechariah 9:9, when a king rides on a donkey, not in violent engagement but in pursuit of peace.

Poetry helps to illuminate the archetypal and subversive aspects of this provocative story. The poetic imagination provides a more incisive rendering of the original narrative:

### What's a King Doing on a Donkey ?

*The Passover feast was a crunch time; Messiahs pretending were rife.*
*And credentials for kingship were checking to ensure the divine would survive.*
*I felt I should do something drastic, this cult so perverse interrupt.*
*So, I opted to ride on a donkey, declaring royal kingship corrupt.*

*Our kings always rode on their horses, the stallion a symbol of power!*
*But the beast of my people for riding was the donkey they used every hour.*
*For threshing, for ploughing and for journeying, and chores by the dozen as well.*
*The donkey empowered their existence, a symbol no one could not excel.*

*The regime of power is redundant, demolished as circles entwine.*
*The center empowers a new freedom with the donkey as icon sublime.*
*And the people cast garlands rejoicing, acclaiming that the God who sets free*
*From the power of the horsemen so brutal, it's the dawn of a new liberty.*

*They accused me of rousing the people. They said they were shouting too loud.*
*When the people befriend new empowerment, even stones hard as rock will*
*cry out.*
*I headed straight up for the temple, the old dispensation locate.*
*And broke through their gross desecration, declaring new ways to relate.*

*The Gospels distorted the story, the task of empowerment subdued.*
*Unique among parable breakthrough, they cut out the poetry of truth.*
*Watch out for that king on the donkey, a symbol prophetic if rare.*
*Declaring that hope still has meaning for those with the courage to dare.*

In this incident, Jesus unambiguously denounces and dis-
owns kingship, and does so with provocative, prophetic symbolism. In a sense, this daring act can be seen as the culmination
of several other subversive acts that characterize his earthly
ministry: particularly, his solidarity with social outcasts in table-
fellowship, his disregard for the restrictions of ritual purity,
his transgression of Sabbath observance, his parabolic stories
stretching conventional moral boundaries sometimes beyond
recognition, his liberating compassion for sinner and the heart-
broken, his cleansing of temple exploitation.[8] The conventional
culture he inherited was in the process of being turned up-side-
down. Power was undermined in the most blatant of ways, and a
new dawn for empowering liberation began to radiate for those
ready to espouse it.

## King of the Land

As already indicated, many of the parables focus on the land, its
usurpation by foreign domination, and the eco-justice required
for its Torah-based retrieval. Edward Said (1993, 77) makes an
astute observation on the critical role of imagination, for the
retrieval in question:

> If there is anything that radically distinguishes the imagination of anti-imperialism, it is the primacy of the geographical in it. . . .The history of colonial servitude is inaugurated by the loss of locality to the outsider. . . . Because of the presence of the colonizing outsider, the land is recoverable at first only through imagination."

Awakening imagination is the primary function of all the Gospel parables, and in many cases, the hearers are invited to imagine new and daring ways in which they can firstly, expose brutal invasion of the alien occupying force, and then revision how it can be returned to its original legitimate owners. Far from being stories articulating fidelity to a patriarchal God-figure (typically depicted as a king), the parables invite rebellion, subversion and deviant imagination, to reclaim the stolen land, precisely because it is the sacred space where the people first encounter the living God, the source of their life and nourishment.

There are several subtleties in the parabolic analysis of the land-crisis in first century Palestine. First of all, is the deep desire to dislodge the foreign invader, and the understandable anger and rage when the colonizer robs the land from the person who understands the land to be God's primary gift for the people's nurturance and growth. The temptation to take up weapons and attempt to oust the invader is very strong, and therefore the temptation to collude with the cycle of violence is very real (see Crossan 2010, 163ff). We see this dynamic played out in Mk.12: 1-12, often described as the Parable of the wicked tenants, frequently allegorized as the Jewish renegades who reject firstly the prophets and then Jesus himself. In its original context, as suggested by Herzog (1994, 108ff), this is more likely a parabolic exposition of the violent cycle – initiated by the colonial invader, but frequently co-opted by the colonized. Such co-option actually undermines the energy for alternative non-violent thinking, luring the victim into deeper paralysis. The parabolic attempt at surfacing prophetic truth is probably best accessed by the poetic imagination:

## *Unmasking the Spiral of Violence*

*There was once a man who planted a vineyard,*
*The land he robbed from a peasant farmer*
*And secured his plunder with a fence of armor.*

*He molds the slaves into zealous tenants,*
*And to some entrusts the task of caring*
*While he goes abroad to exploit sea-faring.*

*But the tenants know that the land they're working*
*Is theirs by right for subsistence living!*
*And against the odds they'll attempt retrieving.*

*For three years running they'll revolt in protest*
*And outwit those sent to collect the produce,*
*But the fourth year running they must clench the surplus.*

*The man's own son, the future owner,*
*Confronts the tenants to declare his tenure*
*In a violent show-down, but who's the winner?*

*The desperation of a brave revolting,*
*To retrieving the land of divine bestowing!*
*But the violent spiral has its own undoing.*

*The elite has force to crush rebellion*
*And the violent spiral reaps a new destruction,*
*In an endless cycle that begets repression.*

*The path to freedom seeks another outlet*
*Beyond the violence of distorted options.*
*Non-violent hope seeks another conscience.*

*The breakthrough comes at another level,*
*Beyond the lure of collusive violence,*
*Awaiting hope with a mystic's presence.*

The hope that engenders the breakthrough carries an inevitable ambiguity, something akin to the ambivalence described in postcolonial theory. We note this in the often misconstrued parable of the talents (Matt.25:14-30) frequently proclaimed within a capitalistic context with God rewarding the exploitive hoarders and condemning the one who chose not to collude with the imperial system. On a surface interpretation, the person with the one talent certainly seems ambivalent, even cowardly – until we investigate more deeply and see the malicious power games being played out.

Contrary to the popular interpretation of *talent*, as personal endowment (or giftedness), in its original historical context the word denotes a financial measurement, the equivalent of fifteen years wages for an average worker. Five talents, therefore, amounts to 75 years wages, while two talents equals 30 years wages. The parable is being told in a social context where the vast majority of people don't have the security of even an annual wage, and where many people would also recognize the betrayal of the socialistic value-system required by Torah, basically despising all practices of usury.

Many of the early Western philosophers including Plato, Aristotle, Cato, Cicero, Seneca and Plutarch were critics of usury. In the legal reforms of the Roman Republic (340 BC), usury and interest were banned. However, in the final period of the Republic, the practice was common. Under Julius Caesar (49-44

BCE), a limit of *12 per cent* was imposed due to the great number of debtors and under Justinian it was set at a mean between 4 per cent and 8 per cent. Even the Romans denounced excessive profiteering, highlighting the highly subversive nature of the parable of the talents, unambiguously denouncing the Empire, its greed and exploitation.

We are dealing with a highly subversive narrative evoking shock and disgust in the hearers, encouraging them to become proactive in the pursuit of eco-justice. The alternative they are offered – the person with the one talent – is indeed ambivalent, but with a prophetic twist that enhances further the subversive intent. He chooses not to collude with the financial exploitation. He opts to become the whistle-blower, calling the brutal landlord to accountability, while exposing the shameful underhand tactics. And there is the subtle dimension to the idea that he buries the talent in the ground which most commentators miss entirely.

How does one bury the equivalent of fifteen years wages in the ground? We are dealing with a cartload of gold or silver. It is not just a case of hiding a small quantity of money to keep it safe – which a lot of people would have done at the time of Jesus. Although there is no textual clue to another interpretation, I wish to suggest the subversive vision of the parable is much better served by describing the third person's response as that of *investing the money in the land* - exactly what the Torah required and recommended. Now the one commonly portrayed as lazy and fearful emerges as a prophetic liberator with cutting edge potential. Of course, he will pay the ultimate price, but his story becomes part of the dangerous memory which in time will undermine even the mighty Empire itself.

We must not subdue his voice, as popular preachers often do. Instead, we need to create outlets for his story to be told. Poetry may be one of the more effective tools:

## *The Parable of the Prophetic Whistleblower*

*The preachers denounce me and moralists trounce me.*
*They judge me unfaithful, a traitor to power.*
*A vilified agent and the money I wasted.*
*I have lived in the shadows of awful repute.*
*Despite the rejection, no roof nor protection*
*I stand by my choice the whistle to blow.*
*I'm anti-corruption and against exploitation.*
*I don't play the games of financial repute.*

*It's time for some testing of the Capital system,*
*The reckless increasing of money to score.*
*The joy of their master means justice disaster*
*As the prowlers of profit consume all before.*

*I waste not nor squander, and my spending I ponder.*
*I sow where I reap, it's the best I can do.*
*But the Capital savage must pursue the ravage*
*And scapegoat the one whose whistle he blew.*

*The Jesus who spoke it and the Church that invoked it*
*Have failed to connect to the heart of the tale.*
*To call the subversive and remain decisive*
*Was the message of Jesus in original lore.*

*Like wealth that allures us, the story pursues us.*
*The subversive truth we oft domesticate.*
*But the New Reign of Jesus marks another excursus*
*Where the one with the whistle holds a prophetic place.*

Postcolonial literature seeks to unravel and challenge the residue of colonial power. Political, economic, social, systemic and personal examples are readily found across the contemporary world. All the world religions carry remnants of such oppression, and all religions show evidence of intransigent attachment to imperial divine power. Engaging such religious elements with rational discourse is not likely to unseat forces that have become deeply embedded over time. Nor is spiritual discernment on its own likely to be more successful. Only strategies with that rare combination of subversion and imagination – as evidenced in the Gospel parables – are likely to deliver the enduring freedom which all humans desire. More on the parables in the next Chapter.

## Crucifying a King

Kwok Pui-Lan (2005, 183) picks up on a critical question posed by the feminist critic Judith Butler (1997): "How can the subjection of a person become the most defining characteristic in the subject formation process?" Why must salvation be postulated on death rather than on life? Why must redemption require so much humiliating pain and torture? Why must suffering be so endemic to personal salvation?

Postcolonial wisdom detects a dangerous and deviant dynamic at work. Patriarchy, like other forms of colonization, is engrossed in the exercise and imposition of power and control. People are perceived to be a threat, and therefore must be kept in their place at all costs. Now if people, can be subdued by inculcating guilt, shame and unworthiness, it will be easier to exert control. If people can be deluded into thinking that suffering is necessary for progress (read: salvation), then a cult of salvific suffering can be a powerful instrument to aid and abet domination and control. All too quickly people will begin to internalize the dynamic, and suffering for the sake of suffering can readily become an end in itself. We saw something of its insidious influence in Martha's story in Chapter Three above.

Early Christianity is frequently held up as a heroic culture thanks to its many martyrs and heroic ascetics. In the light of Candida Moss's incisive critique (Moss 2013), we begin to understand another manipulative strategy of patriarchal propaganda, invoked to validate and promote domination and control? In a challenging and inspiring study, Brock and Parker (2008), ask why we find no images of crucifixes or scenes of God in judgment anywhere in the Roman catacombs where thousands of Christians were martyred? What we find are several frescoes celebrating the luscious growth of nature through plant and animal life. This imagery reveals another dynamic at work which Brock and Parker claim eluded Christian scholars for much of the past 1,000 years of Christendom (the second Christian millennium).

After the publication of St. Anselm's *Cur Deus?* in 1095, atonement theology came to the fore, focused primarily on God sacrificing his beloved son to procure salvation for sinful humans. In the power of the Cross we were saved, and with it came the grace to enter paradise when we died. Paradise, therefore, denoted life with God in the hereafter, outside and beyond this vale of tears. But it seems that *paradise* had a very different connotation in the first Christian millennium: *it denoted the transformation of this world into God's new creation.* Hence the imagery of nature, so widespread in the Roman catacombs: the martyrs, it seems, did not understand their cruel death as a pathway to paradise in a life beyond, but as the price they were paying to contribute to God's transformative process here on earth – in modern jargon, to help to bring about heaven on earth.

These reflections provide a useful backdrop to our current understanding of the death (and Resurrection) of the historical Jesus. The Mel Gibson portrayal of God's son in torture to save sinful humanity still exerts an extensive appeal particularly to the millions of Christians in our world condemned to poverty and oppression. Like Martha (in Chapter Three), the crucifix remains a potent symbol of power and love. It is an object of devotion – but with a limited potential as a catalyst for transformation and systemic change.

A few facts need to be invoked and honored throughout these reflections:

1. Jesus died because of how he lived. His death is an inevitable consequence of a life fully and radically lived. He so empowered the people of his day, that the colonial powers of the time (Jewish and Roman) could no longer tolerate him. They seized an opportune moment, crucified him, and made sure he would not survive the ordeal.

2. Jesus was *crucified*, a Roman punishment meted out primarily to subversives, to those who challenged the cultural values of power and domination, those who posed a threat to the integrity of religious and political power.

3. Jesus died because he lived and behaved in a highly prophetic way, but it was prophecy at the service of justice and empowerment, and should not be construed as some type of sanctimonious immolation for the salvation of sinners.

4. Jesus suffered – in both his life and death – in order to rid the world of meaningless suffering. Jesus never advocated suffering for its own sake.

5. The Gospel writers glamorize and sensationalize the death of Jesus (as does Mel Gibson in the 21st. century) with an array of trials and miraculous feats. This depiction is based on the evangelists' misconception that Jesus was really an earthly king (endowed with divinity) and therefore would be treated like a king even in death. This royal rhetoric seriously undermines the true nature of what was transpiring.

6. The critical witnesses at the death (and in the transformative events that followed) were a group of women. All the men had fled in fear, lest they too be crucified. 2000 years later Christendom has not yet discerned truly – and consequently has not come to terms with – the crucial role of the female disciples in the final days of the historical Jesus.

7. The Resurrection of Jesus cannot be explained as the resuscitation of a dead corpse. Resurrection is much more about a transformative/mystical experience known primarily to the women disciples. In metaphorical terms Resurrection can be understood as a divine validation and affirmation of a life lived to the full. Consequently, Resurrection is a counterpart to the life of Jesus rather than to the death of Jesus.

8. Christians have grossly exaggerated the death of Jesus as an integral dimension of Christian faith. Much of this inflated claim has to do with the dynamics of power and domination, examined afresh throughout the pages of this book. Christian salvation and redemption belong primarily to the LIFE of Jesus and not merely to his untimely death.

9. The focus on purifying suffering and redemptive violence continues long after the death of Jesus materializing into a cult of martyrdom that dominates early Christian witness to the faith. Both Brock & Parker (2008) and Moss (2013) provide informed and timely critiques on the exaggerated and inflated nature of martyrdom in early Christian times.

Jesus died neither as a king nor as a patriarchal warrior. His untimely death was a colonial act of suppression, to eliminate the threat of a prophetic liberator. His death is an integral dimension of his life and should never be separated from it. Compared with his exemplary life, his quick brutal death offers neither wisdom nor hope, other than serving as another sordid example of colonial oppression. Christianity, for far too long, has engaged in a lurid fascination on meaningless pain and torture. Instead of trying to rid the world of such atrocities, we have sanctioned their existence as tools to subjugate those who disagree with us.

We are caught in a kind of addictive lure to imperial domestication. There is no room for redemptive violence in a faith committed to the Companionship of Empowerment. The age-long collusion between violence and suffering needs to be dissolved, as we confront the dysfunctional sinfulness of our world with a prophetic challenge for justice and empowering hope. Yes, that project will involve suffering, and at times may cost us an untimely death, but its primary focus is life, and the transformation of our world, and not merely an act of sacrificial victimhood to escape to an utopia beyond the sky.

## Resurrecting the Divine Warrior

According to American scholar, Michael R. Licona (2010, 611), the Resurrection of Jesus is the subject of more than 3,400 books and articles written during the past thirty years. Licona's work provides a useful overview, written primarily from a historian's perspective. Another comprehensive overview, employing theological and scientific wisdom is that of Peters et al. (2002). Madigan and Levinson (2008, 192ff) offer valuable insight on how the cultural archetype of the divine warrior influences the interpretation of Jesus's Resurrection. As we have encountered in the life of Jesus, so also in his death and its aftermath, kingly power and glory dominates the landscape and inevitably translates into Jesus triumphing into exalted glory. Thus, the Resurrection becomes the ultimate destiny for Christianity's divine hero, once more leaving liberated incarnational people co-dependent on a glorified exalted rescuer.

Much of the adulation attributed to Jesus in his Resurrection has parallels in other ancient narratives of exalted heroes, a subject requiring further research as intimated by Licona (2010). From Ugaritic sources we have: Baal, Melqart, Adonis, Eshmun, Osiris and Dumuzi. In ancient Greek mythology, Asclepius was killed by Zeus, only to be resurrected and transformed into a major deity. Achilles, after being killed, was snatched from his funeral pyre by his divine mother, Thetis, resurrected and brought to an immortal existence in another domain. The Persian Mithra, the Indian Krishna, and the Buddha are also known to have transcended physical death. According to Jan Assmann (in Peters et al. 2002, 126), Resurrection in Egyptian mythology was an exclusively royal privilege, granting an exonerated breakthrough to the royal one, which non-royals could never hope to attain.[9]

In the Christian story, Jesus is miraculously raised from the dead, in 'bodily' form. According to John's Gospel the Resurrection denotes not merely a miraculous return to life, but is understood theologically as a declaration of Jesus' full exaltation to the royal heights of heaven. Christianity has long understood the Resurrection of Jesus to be proof of his divinity, through which Jesus was able to defy and transcend the power of death and return alive on earth before eventually being taken back into heaven.

Belief in the Resurrection of Jesus still fluctuates between those who take the event literally (the resuscitation of a dead body escaping miraculously from the tomb) and those who regard it as symbolic and metaphoric, describing the experience of the first witnesses rather than anything that happened to Jesus himself. The postcolonial perspective – always suspicious of our tendency to exaggerate and divinize patriarchal power - veers towards the latter position. Postcolonialists are not mere postmodernists, recklessly abandoning inherited conventional truth, nor are they alien to the notion of divine, supernatural action. Their critique is aimed at the tendency to attribute unilateral power to figures like Jesus, thus creating a precedent for extensive disempowerment of all other God-like creatures.

We will never know if the evangelists were influenced by parallel Resurrection stories in Egypt, Greece and elsewhere, but clearly they retain an understanding of Jesus as an imperial divine figurehead, whose eventual glorification they will depict in elaborate miraculous terms. And their primary interest is in Jesus himself, not in what the early followers experienced. I support the analysis of the South African scholar, Pieter Craffert (2008) reminding us that people at the time of Jesus had access to altered states of consciousness (ASC) to a degree largely unknown in our time. The post –Resurrection appearance stories, therefore, may aptly describe the psycho-spiritual experiences of those deeply traumatized by the untimely death of Jesus, having been firstly deeply transformed by his exemplary life. Even if something miraculous did happen to Jesus himself, there seems far more empowering potential in exploring the ramifications for the first believers, despite the fact that we don't have concrete evidence for that outcome.

Viewing the Resurrection as a transformative experience of the early witnesses, also is more congruent and respectful of the empowering subversive One who was snatched away by an untimely death. The whole life of Jesus – and the premature death – had one central goal: the *companionship of empowerment*. There is a postcolonial logic in viewing the Resurrection as an empowering set of visions that re-energized the petrified witnesses and helped to re-group them into a companionship that would embark on the rising of a new covenantal people, and not just focusing on a resurrected divine hero.

## The End of Kingship

The resurrection narrative marks the end of imperial kingship, as the first witnesses are launched on an empowering mission to Galilee (Matt.28:7) – where Jesus first proclaimed the New Reign of God. In the disciples' transformative resurrection experience, we got rid of the imperial king! The male evangelists desperately tried to cling on to the imperial power and glory – as did several subsequent generations of Church leaders – but those who carried Resurrection hope – to Galilee and beyond - were endowed with a different non-imperial, non-violent dream.

All of which leaves the Christian faith today, with an almost insurmountable problem: *we have obliterated the original witnesses.* The first post-Resurrection disciples were not the twelve, nor the seventy-two, but a group of women (which probably did include men) inspired and led by Mary Magdalene. It is that group who kept alive the fire for empowerment; they became the first champions of the new companionship. Long before the twelve returned for Pentecost – if they ever did (see pp.106-107) – the ecclesial empowering community had already been established – not along imperial lines, but as a subversive, egalitarian, empowering community as initially inspired by the living witness of the historical Jesus.

While the Christian Church(es) continues to cling to imperialism, and the cult of kingship, it will remain not merely a Church in crisis, but an idolatrous fabrication, built on false foundations. Jesus never adopted kingship – he forthrightly denounced it in all its vestiges. The risen Christ, embodied in the first disciples, transcended the colonial residue. The non-imperial foundations were firmly established, and sooner or later, the Christian faith-community must come to terms with that subversive fact.

Scripture scholar, Elizabeth Schussler Fiorenza, threw down the gauntlet in 1983, with the publication of her seminal work, *In*

*Memory of Her.* She built on the ground work of earlier decades, and was followed by a plethora of professional studies on the role of women in the Gospels and in early Christian times (cf. Kramer & d'Angelo 1999; Bauckham 2002; Cooper 2013). The truth too long subverted is beginning to haunt the Christian community. It is a matter of time till we reach the postcolonial critical mass. And then the radiant truth of the Gospel will illuminate what we have for too long preached, but not practiced: Seek FIRST the New Reign of God and its justice . . . and all the rest will fall into place (cf. Matt.6:33).

# Chapter 6:
# *Postcolonial Empowerment: Word and Action*

*The constant challenge a postcolonial critic faces is how to maintain marginal status. How to be on the edge. How to remain an outsider.*

R.S. Sugirtharajah

*This is an intervention. A message from that space in the margin that is a site of creativity and power, that inclusive space where we recover ourselves, where we meet in solidarity to erase the category colonized/colonizer. Marginality is the space [site] of resistance. Enter that space. Let us meet there. Enter that space. We greet you as liberators.*

bell hooks

For far too long the Christian churches have viewed the life and ministry of Jesus as a divine intervention into a flawed, secular reality, impacting upon humans as the primary victims of the dysfunctional world order. The intervention was mediated by divinely-infused kingship, known in Christian rhetoric as divine messiahship. Only a certain sector of society were deemed 'worthy' to befriend the divine intervention: namely elite, educated males. The hegemonic power belonged primarily, if not exclusively, to the elite male sub-group. For the rest – comprising a possible 90% of the rank-and-file of society – people belonged to the 'outside' – subalterns to one degree or another.

Liberation theology, in the late twentieth century, tried to recapture the Gospel as the hope of the poor and marginalized. Striving to highlight the plight of the poor in social, systemic and economic terms, the movement ran amok of an imperial Church petrified of any ecclesial movement promoting personal and social empowerment. The movement also suffered an internal weakness as it failed to name succinctly the colonizing forces that created such poverty in the first place, and the globalized corporations that sustain the oppression today. Instead of being accused of being too 'secular', the movement stands accused of not being secular enough.

While portraying a Jesus strongly in solidarity with the poor and marginalized, liberation theology failed to highlight the subversive empowerment fundamental to Christian faith. In its often strong alignment with popular devotions, and charismatic fervor, the praxis of liberation endorsed the devotion of consolation rather than the spirituality of liberation. While creating theological horizons far in excess of conventional Christianity, liberation theology still lacks the dangerous subversive rhetoric of New Testament parable and miracle. This is the postcolonial contribution I wish to explore in the present Chapter.

## Subaltern Marginalization

Postcolonial theory identifies subalterns as a central focus for rehabilitation and empowerment. 'Subaltern' originally is a term for subordinates in military hierarchies and was first used in a non-military sense by the Marxist, Antonio Gramsci. In current postcolonial studies, it refers to any person or group of inferior rank and station, whether because of race, class, gender, sexual orientation, ethnicity or religion. Some thinkers use it in a general sense to refer to marginalized groups, deprived of agency, social status, and political representation, thus unable to access the benefits if the dominant culture (Gayatri Chakravorty Spivak). Homi Bhabha also applies the term to oppressed minority groups whose presence was crucial to the self-definition of the majority group. Other theorists use the term for those individuals and movements which resist the hegemonic power of modern globalization.

Subaltern groups and individuals populate the Gospel texts. Those depicted as disempowered – the poor, the marginalized, the sick, those physically impaired, and those afflicted by evil spirits – tend to be cast in a co-dependent relationship with Jesus, as the one who rescues and heals them with a power totally outside and beyond their reach. Echoes abound of people being incapacitated because of their failure to abide by divine law and guidance. Contemporary analysis of sickness and suffering at the time indicate quite a different cultural context, with external oppression (Roman and Jewish) debilitating people and disempowering them often to the point of physical illness, or psychological insanity. In which case, the healing miracles are not merely about human restoration to health and well-being, but a postcolonial critique of those systemic cultural forces that impacted so destructively on people and their well-being.

A vivid example is that of Lk.8:1-3:

> And it so happened soon afterward that he travelled through the towns and villages, preaching and announcing the good news of the kingdom of God. The twelve were with him, and also some women whom he had cured of evil spirits and diseases: Mary, called Magdalene, from whom seven demons had gone out, and Joanna, the wife of Chusa, Herod's steward, and Susanna, and many others, who provided for them out of their needs.

The women are explicitly named whereas the male followers are not, and the reader can easily be left with a complementary sense of the women's importance, providing for Jesus and the apostles out of their means. Until we note the status of their leader, Mary of Magdala, inflicted with evil spirits and infirmities. The men are good, but the women are problematic. For Luke, is the connection of Chuza with King Herod also problematic? From a postcolonial perspective, Chuza's role could be considered highly prophetic, a mole in the patriarchal system; it is unlikely that Luke views her in this light. Overall, the text suggests that the women are subalterns, valued for their domestic support, while the males are agents in the primary work of the Kingdom as preachers and teachers.

This is not merely a status of oppression as we understand it today. In early Christian times, the arrangement was understood as something much closer to a divine mandate. God had chosen it to be this way. In the divine economy of salvation, creation is flawed so that God's glory can be manifested through its salvific transformation, and in that process the male elite have the primary role. This quickly translated into male apostles, male priests, and the gradual evolution of a presbyterate, prioritizing the male sex.

We also need to note the beleaguered status of the land itself, demoted from being God's great gift to the people, according to the covenantal imperative of the Hebrew Scripture. Not merely do the Romans rob the land from its primary owners – the subject of several parables, as reviewed later in this Chapter – but it appears that the collusive Jewish authorities do little to defend their own people from such marauding invasion. The issue at stake here is not just ownership and right to usufruct. What is under threat is a type of organic conviviality, described in vivid detail by the naturalist, David Abram (2011). People's identity, the daily raison d'etre that grounds both their faith in God, and meaning in life, is intimately and inseparably inter-woven with the organicity of the land itself. And that organic sacredness is now colonized, usurped and corrupted.

Into this flawed divinely-imperial culture comes the historical Jesus. His arrival on earth is by a miraculous birth (as with several other messianic figures of the time), with heavenly esoteric beings (angels), i.e., royal representatives, acclaiming his arrival. As indicated in a previous Chapter, his royal line of descent is checked out and verified by both Matthew and Luke. And even at a young age he is acclaimed to be full of wisdom and maturity (Lk.2:46-52), a royal portent in the making!

We can only speculate what his youth and adolescence were like – probably a restless spiritual seeker that caused no small measure of stress to his family and local community. He seems to have joined the millenarian movement of John the Baptist, with its distinctive apocalyptic focus of fasting and penance. Gradually he realized that his call was to something different, so he abandoned John to espouse a highly controversial strategy characterized by feasting, healing and empowerment of the masses. It seems he never married, thus setting himself up as a subaltern causing embarrassment and stress to his family and friends.[10]

Eventually, he began to move in the public domain primarily in the villages and small towns of Israel. The one time Baptist vagabond became a subversive subaltern. The Gospels suggest that he frequently invoked an esoteric message described in English (from the Greek) as the *Kingdom of God*, better rendered today as the *Companionship of Empowerment*: a non-violent revolution turning kingship on its head, and perhaps for the first time in ancient history casting doubt and ridicule on the divine prerogative of kingship itself. It was an attack not merely on the power-base of Judaism, but on the world-wide religious culture upon which the sacred nature of patriarchy grew and flourished. It was a paradigm shift of enormous proportion!

This new king would prove to be a radically disturbing subversive. He would shift consciousness through liberating narratives, restorative justice, holistic healing, revolutionary table-fellowship, unconditional forgiveness, and non-violent rehabilitation of the land. He would break rules, sacred and secular alike. He would gather vagabonds into circles of friendship without boundary or limit. And all for one purpose: *to establish on earth a culture of mutual empowerment that would undermine every imperial regime that humanity had ever known.*

## When a King Tells Stories

In the ascending Greek culture of early Christianity, Aristotle's influence can scarcely be underrated. Not surprisingly, it became the basis of scholastic philosophy several centuries later. For Aristotle, human authenticity is defined by several qualities but to the fore is the power of human reason. Intelligent people use their heads to figure things out, and in human discourse, rational, reasonable argument is indicative of a civilized, progressive culture.

The disciples were baffled and confused by Jesus' frequent adoption of this new strategy of the Companionship of Empowerment (Kingdom of God) —so were the disciples of John the Baptist, and particularly the Pharisees. Not surprisingly, therefore, Jesus is often asked for an explanation – particularly by the Pharisees. Typically, Jesus answers their concern not by a logical, coherent explanation (as one would expect from a culture of rationality), but by telling highly subversive stories, that scramble their neat conceptual view of reality and leave them reeling in confusion and frustration. We enter the paradoxical world of parabolic lore.

Although Jesus employed the idea of parable narrative as a means of inculcating his message more extensively and more effectively than any other teacher, he did not invent the parable. The parable was employed both in the Old Testament (five times) and in contemporaneous Jewish literature. And in the one attempt to explain to the followers what parables meant (Mk.4:11-13), those offered the explanation must have been more baffled than ever:

> And he said to them: To you has been given the secret of the kingdom of God, but for those outside everything is in parables; so that they may indeed see but not perceive, and may indeed hear but not understand, lest they turn again and be forgiven. And he said to them: do you not understand this parable? How then will you understand all the parables?

Widely recognized as one of the most difficult texts in the New Testament, it clearly asserts that:
a) parables embody ambiguity and paradox transcending the human mode of rational explanation and, therefore,
b) the parable requires a mode of hearing and understanding based on discerning wisdom rather than conventional human comprehension.

The message being conveyed – whether to an immediate group of obtuse disciples, or to seekers after meaning in later Christian times – is not accessible to rational explanation. And any attempt at a rational explanation of the parables will sell short their empowering subversive wisdom. Poetry stands a much better chance of opening up the horizon of promise and hope, inviting a contemplative gaze rather than the penetrating analysis of the rational mind.

## _The Parable of Enlightened Confusion_

*The stories Jesus told them turned their world upside-down,*
*Bombarding every certainty they knew.*
*The boundaries were disrupted,*

*Their sacred creeds corrupted,*
*Every hope they had constructed*
*Was questioned to the core!*
*By the time the story ended,*
*Stretching meaning so distended,*
*On one truth their life depended,*
*What they'd known for long before.*

*Some disciples who were ready he called them to one side,*
*Inviting them to risk a dream come true.*
*Companions for empowerment,*
*A sacred new endowment,*
*Ready for a new announcement,*
*The breakthrough long proclaimed.*
*Those yet who cannot see it,*
*No riddles to perceive it,*
*Confused they only flee it,*
*And cling on to ancient lore.*

*The connection with Isaiah he thought might do the trick,*
*Their hist'ry might illuminate the way.*
*Unless the eye is open wide,*
*Unless the ear echoes from inside,*
*Unless the heart risks to confide,*
*You'll miss the haunting truth.*
*Like seeds that fall upon the ground,*
*Some parched and lost cannot rebound,*
*Yet much will flourish tall and sound,*
*And yield one-hundred fold.*

*It's a text of ambiguity, true to parabolic lore,*
*Disrupting every certainty we hold.*
*With the scholars out of season,*

*There's another way to reason,*
*And to some it feels like treason,*
*To the powers who long control.*
*So embrace new liberation,*
*In the heart of God's creation,*
*And in storied proclamation,*
*Let the seeds of hope sprout forth.*

A vast literature exists on the parables. While scholars still debate precise meaning and methods of interpretation, there is widespread agreement on these factors:

- Parables as told by Jesus have a distinctive subversive flavor with few precedents in ancient Hebrew literature. These are stories that challenge and disturb several sanctioned cultural and moral norms.
- Parables stretch conventional wisdom to breaking point - and beyond.
- Parables leave the hearer with dislocated feelings and major conceptual adjustments.
- Parables resolve nothing; rather they open up reality into a vast new range of fresh possibilities.
- All the parables require inclusiveness of previously excluded dimensions of life.
- The parables break through the dualistic split between sacred and secular.

Remarkably, few commentators highlight the radical departure from the cultural expectation of the day, namely, that responsible males (particularly) strive to employ the rational and reasonable rhetoric of the prevailing Greek culture. Jesus blatantly flies in the face of this expectation. Secondly, few truly honor the subversive tenor of these stories – William

Herzog (1994) being one of the notable exceptions. And thirdly, the adult dimension of such story-engagement is rarely acknowledged.

Catechists try to simplify parable stories to make them more accessible to children (preachers tend to do the same thing), when in fact, Jesus used such stories to engage adult followers in adult-based discipleship in the service of an adult God. *The call to mature adulthood is written all over the parabolic landscape.* To honor the subversive intent, along with its adult challenge, the following elements need more discerning attention:

1. The Gospel writers themselves seem to have departed significantly from the original purpose of the parables as told by Jesus.

2. The Gospel writers – or other editors – tend to spiritualize and moralize the original stories undermining their foundational political, economic and spiritual counter-culture.

3. The tendency to allegorize the parables (make ethical and/or spiritual comparisons) frequently undermines and distorts the liberating empowerment of the original story.

4. Interpretations that equate Jesus (or God) with the leading character (the king, the landlord), not merely distract from the foundational message, but mark a serious departure from the non-imperial vision of the New Reign of God.

5. Colonial mimicry – depicting God or Jesus as an imperial figure – features in many of the parables stories. This is more likely to be an editorial outcome rather than behavior adopted by the historical Jesus.

6. Many parables adopt dualistic splitting (sheep v. goats; wise v. foolish virgins), a literary and cultural tactic of the time that the Hebrew Jesus is unlikely to have used.

Many of these distortions can be seen in the parable of the workers in the vineyard (Matt.20:1-16), in which the landlord is frequently depicted as God, exemplifying a sense of justice and generosity that defies the normative practice of paying people in accordance with the service they have rendered. When one better understands the exploitative employment practices of the time, and the precarious plight of the expendables (cf. Herzog 1994; Horsley 2008), then we expose the blatant exploitation and economic oppression embodied in this narrative. In the name of the Companionship of Empowerment, another interpretation is needed, one more likely to be congruent with the historical Jesus as champion of the poor and oppressed. And poetry is likely to immerse us more viscerally in the desire for justice and liberation, as evoked by the original story:

*Outing the Roots of Exploitation*

*The landlord needs the laborers his harvest to procure.*
*How many needed for the task, he clearly is unsure.*
*The daily wage he offers each, subsistence, 'twill provide,*
*but may not clear the debts accrued in a culture so contrived.*
*Amid the heat and sweat of toil the workers undertake,*
*ensuring all is gathered in, a harvest rich they'll make.*
*And glad they are at eventide, awaiting recompense,*
*sustain their meagre struggling hearts 'gainst poverty's defence.*

*And what a shock-encounter, they can scarcely entertain*
*the brutal vitriolic of a reckless renegade.*

125

*"You take what I am offering, the measure I declare,*
*to challenge my integrity no one on earth should dare."*
*The colonizing system is once again exposed*
*as workers face corruption, a bitter truth disclosed.*
*The justice voice of protest rings out a piercing chill,*
*despite the power against them, the workers wont stand still.*

*This parable we must not yield to superficial gloss,*
*a God-like figure generous, equality so gross.*
*Instead expose subversively, the truth to conscientize,*
*empowering those whose hearts are crushed, rebellious spirits rise.*
*The Gospel of non-violence, a truth profound declare:*
*collude not any person with oppression so unfair.*
*And rally colleagues waiting, companions to empower,*
*one day the just will claim the earth – the vineyard's finest hour!*

From a postcolonial perspective, power is totally turned upside down. Empowerment emerges with daring new possibilities. All the parable stories reflect local domestic issues, inviting the participants to stop looking to the morbid empire which can never deliver genuine breakthrough, but look instead to wisdom from the base upward. Empowerment is fused from collective, mutual mobilization, and not from reliance on top-down imperialism, earthly or divine. And that empowerment becomes even more dynamic when we explore the complex territory of the Gospel miracles.

Many of the parables vividly illustrate that empowering breakthrough, eg., the stories of the widow's mite and the widow challenging the judge (see pp. 27-28 above), but what do we make of the steward who swindles the books to his advantage (Lk.16:1-9)? This subversive tale pushes many moral guidelines to a breaking point. Is Jesus actually encouraging the oppressed one to play the powergame to his own advantage? Survival at any cost? Parables do not give rational answers to such questions, and they certainly don't offer moral directives. But they provoke us to think, to imagine, and conjure up alternative possibilities. And perhaps only a trans-rational rhetoric – the subliminal poetic imagination - can captivate the subtle prophetic core of such a challenging and disturbing parable:

*Wise as Serpents & Clever as . . .*

*Where is there poetry in swindling the books*
*Where is there ethics in dealing with crooks?*
*Where is God's Kingdom at work in the tale,*
*Empowering a new dispensation!*

*What hope is left when a steward is dismissed;*
*Is there one honest way in which he can resist?*
*Is it right to resort to survive at all costs*
*Empowering a new dispensation!*

*Might shrewdness and prudence be considered well*
*To live like a Christian, despair to dispel?*
*The system transgresses through wile and through wit*
*Empowering a new dispensation.*

*Could this be a parable for God's Reign breakthrough*
*Disrupting the neatness that ethics construe?*
*And who's right or wrong, while justice procure*
*Empowering a new dispensation!*

*Is Jesus declaring the steward got it right*
*Despite playing such tactics exemplifies light?*
*To bring greater justice – is no price too great*
*So that God's Reign can break in and flourish?*

*So counter-intuitive this parable wit,*
*Disrupting convention with passion and grit!*
*When your back's to the wall, and your corner'd all round*
*Remember the swindler who broke through!*

## Ever Heard of a King who Heals?

Alternatively, we can view parables and miracles as two expressions or articulations of the promised breakthrough. The parable of the creative story questions the prevailing assumptions, shatters the power-based rhetoric, and evokes new imaginative constructs for thought and speech. The parable of the symbolic action (miracle) conscientizes those trapped by internalized oppression, and in the power of healing and compassion shows how people can be set free from the bondage of oppression.

The tendency to spiritualize the miracle stories, and view them primarily as deeds of divine power, undermines the significance of the social, economic, and political factors, that give substance and passion to the narratives. Only when we embrace this wider disciplinary base, can we access a fuller understanding on how the miracle activity of Jesus contributes proactively to the Companionship of Empowerment.

The Gospels describe three different categories of miracles: healings (including exorcisms), overcoming natural limitation; raising from the dead. For the purposes of the present work, I confine my observations to the healing miracles. Illness, pain and suffering in the time of Jesus suggested a lack of equilibrium with the surrounding spirit-infused culture. Sickness could be caused by an infringement of social, interpersonal norms and expectations. For instance, the norms of ritual purity led to exclusions and social labelling that would sound meaningless in the Western world today. And the bio-medical approach to human illness, pain and suffering was largely unknown in that epoch.

128

Medicine in the time of Jesus was predominantly herbal in nature. Often the herbal treatments were expensive, so substantial numbers of people would use natural remedies or turn to local healers (as in the case of healing witchcraft in Africa today). The healers often followed the shamanistic tradition of trance and the use of rituals, possibly using clay, water, extract from native plants, human saliva, or other body fluids, as South African scholar, Pieter F. Craffert (2008, 245-308) comprehensively demonstrates. Scholars seem loath to explore these alternative healing methodologies which were extensively used in ancient societies. The fear seems to be that we might undermine the unique supernatural power of Jesus - and of God. One wonders if this fear arises from unresolved colonial indoctrination, along with the ensuing concern that it might weaken the teaching authority of official churches.

Could it be the same preoccupation with the supernatural that fuels the legalistic denunciation of those who don't approve of what Jesus is doing, particularly on the Sabbath? Is there a colonial influence at work whereby we must not allow the all-perfect, all-powerful divine One to deviate from even the minutiae of prescribed divine law, in this case Sabbath observance? The Pharisees, Levites and priests seem to be unduly preoccupied lest Jesus might deviate from sacred law; those who see themselves as entrusted with divine patrimony might be in danger of being usurped by others, whose only access to the divine should be mediated by specially chosen ones, eg., the temple priesthood. This petrified preoccupation becomes all the more transparent through poetic insight:

*They Watched Him Closely* (Luke 14:1)

*They watched and they wondered*
*What he might get up to next!*

129

*Keep a close eye on the bastard.*
*He's rousing up our people*
*With all these signs and wonders.*
*And dangerous subversive stories*
*Empowering renegades and rebels,*
*As they gather round tables where*
*Every law is flouted and raucous revelry*
*Disturbs on a daily basis the power of Pax Romana.*

*They watched and they wondered:*
*What does the Sabbath mean for this bastard?*
*He's supposed to be of God,*
*Kingly blood from Davidic background,*
*Messianic pedigree, they claim.*
*And his family are obedient, law-abiding folks.*
*Yet, he causes his family daily embarrassment,*
*He won't get married or settle down*
*A restless vagabond, an utopian wreck,*
*And a definite threat to the power of Pax Romana.*

*They watched and they wondered:*
*The people claim he's a magical healer*
*And that he cures the blind and lame.*
*But worst of all he usurps our priestly power*
*As if God's forgiveness was a free-for-all.*
*The cheeky bastard questions our sacred wisdom*
*And quotes the prophets with arrogant disrespect.*
*A new reign of God let loose he claims,*
*With everyone in and no more outside,*
*A hell of an insult to the power of Pax Romana.*

*They watched and they wondered:*
*This motley gang attracting fisher-folk,*

*And allegedly some women, endowed with crucial role.*
*And to the fore, a shady character of famed repute,*
*A cherished confidante - from Magdala no less!*
*This bastard does things differently,*
*We must watch his every move*
*And set whatever traps we can to halt*
*His devious empowerment - must never pose a threat*
*To the order of God's rule, the power of Pax Romana.*

At a later stage, the Christian church often interpreted the miracles as a proof for the divinity of Jesus, and his power to intervene miraculously on behalf of co-dependent, flawed humans. From both an anthropological and Christological point of view, this interpretation smacks of colonial oppression. We evidence a classical dualism between the all-powerful God and the totally powerless human person. The Jesus we encounter is a pale shadow of the empowering catalyst of the new companionship (the Kingdom), and so passively dependent are humans, they stand little chance of engaging collaboratively with the Companionship of Empowerment. Instead, co-dependent projections abound, attributing to Jesus' king-like divine miraculous power, exalting his king-like supremacy over all aspects of human life, especially sickness and oppression.

There are other ways to discern the spiritual and cultural significance of the miracle narratives. As indicated in a previous work (O'Murchu 2011, 74ff), I suggest a two-pronged approach to the miracle stories. Firstly, that we view the miracles as *parables in action*, the challenge therefore being to surface the subversive and paradoxical message within the word-event. And, secondly, that we pay close attention to *internalized oppression* as the critical issue being exposed and addressed in many of these episodes.

When the Gospels describe people as being blind, deaf, dumb, maimed, crippled, bent over and even dead, is it not likely

131

that we are encountering psycho-somatic deprivation possibly arising from social, economic and political disempowerment? Similarly with the stories of exorcisms; might these not be narratives of people driven insane because of the oppression of Roman occupation, the usurpation of land, the burden of taxation, social and personal dislocation. Several commentators have noted the abundant use of military language in Mark's story of the Gerasene demoniac (Mk.5:1-20), suggesting he was driven insane because of brutality ensuing from Roman oppression. (See the comprehensive overview of Anna Runesson 2011, 186-212).

The story of the Gerasene demoniac carries strong connotations of internalized oppression. Possibly stripped of his land, driven into poverty, unable to pay debts or taxes, a social outcast even within his own family ranks, this is a person whose demented spirit could well have led to a severe psychotic breakdown. A classical contemporary example of internalized oppression is the strategy adopted by the Zimbabwean president, Robert Mugabe, in his treatment of his own people. Mugabe contributed to the removal of the British colonizers from his native land. He helped to displace the external oppressor. Several years later, his regime within Zimbabwe, sought to reclaim land from white farmers, brutalizing thousands as the external oppressors (the British) had done to the black people 50-100 years previously. This was not merely an act of revenge, because it was activated in such a way that millions of black people also suffered significantly. Robert Mugabe had helped throw out the external oppressor, but he had not expelled from his heart the residue of imperial terror, and, consequently, his internalized oppression, took a toll on his own people – black and white – as severe as any brutality exerted by the external oppressor in former times.

What are often described in the Gospels as exorcisms – with heavy emphasis on expelling evil spirits – may well be a first century rendering of what today we understand as internalised oppression. Anna Runesson (2011, 211) makes this astute observation:

> Not only do Jesus' exorcisms deal directly with the subject of colonial oppression; they address the problem more to the point than would a straightforward confrontation between the Messiah and the Roman generals. Far from treating the symptom without addressing the disease, Jesus' exorcisms cut directly to the heart of the matter, even if a single exorcism leaves much more work to be done.

It is much easier to expel the external oppressor rather than undo the grip of internalized oppression. The former is overt and conscious, the latter is covert and deeply subconscious. A person, a group, or even a nation can convey a strong semblance of being externally free, while still harbouring within the crippling residue of a subjected people. People who have been abused – physically, mentally, sexually - can bury deep inside – for several years – the experience of their abuse. It is consigned to a hidden woundedness that will never heal while it is buried so deeply. And it can be very scary to allow such dangerous stuff to come to the surface.

In fact, it is nearly always a life crisis or trauma, that brings the repressed material to the surface. And long before that will happen, people are likely to suffer various illnesses for which there may be no obvious explanation. The aetiology of the sickness is beyond the purvey of the rational senses, and often beyond the skill of conventional medicine. It is repressed, internalized pain breaking out, irrationally, chaotically, and often unpredictably. The raw pain can no longer be contained, and it finds its own outlet in disease, illness, trauma, and possible insanity.

Jesus portrayed as a conventional king has no answer for this dilemma, other than to invoke his divine supremacy to subvert the oppression. In turn, this breeds further co-dependency. The so-called 'healing' is a perverse strategy to exert dominance and control. It fails to empower the wounded one to become proactive towards self-healing and self-empowerment. It is alien to the whole spirit of the Companionship of Empowerment and alien as well to what authentic redeemed humanity is all about.

Throughout the Gospels, men and women alike suffer from various ailments that manifest as blindness, deafness, being dumb or crippled. Adopting a literal interpretation is likely to short-circuit a more complex and deeper meaning, as we glean from a poetic purvey of the man with the withered hand (Mk.3:1-6; Lk.6:6-11).

### *The Symbolic Subversion of a Withered Hand*

*It looks as if they're furious because of one empowered;*
*There's something more than Sabbath law at stake.*
*It's empowerment for the people,*
*Which the system made so feeble,*
*Whether maimed or blind or cripple,*
*The prison chains are broke.*
*And the powers will be suspicious*
*When the people rise ambitious,*
*Every move is deemed seditious,*
*Empowerment's healing force.*
*And to have it all transpiring on a holy Sabbath day*
*Is just too much to take in as tension soars in fray.*

*The withered hand's a symbol for rising power subdued*
*And the right hand been disabled is the crux.*
*Deprived of basic dignity,*

*Derided by nobility*
*Long days without activity*
*Will destroy the human soul.*
*For the powers, it's useful to restrain*
*And keep the masses with tight rein,*
*Control requires the plight of pain*
*To quell empowerment's force.*
*And the Sabbath is a good day to drive the message home*
*That those who claim to know God's will no longer overcome.*

*But Jesus rallies hope anew,*
*Prophetic grace once more break through*
*All hands on deck empowering forth.*
*The branch that withered in Autumn's fall*
*Will bloom again in the Springtime call.*
*And the one whose hand has been restored*
*Will shake the empire to its very core!*

As parables in action, the symbolic intent of the miracle stories is likely to beget a more profound discernment. Understood at this deeper level, every word and deed of the historical Jesus serves the liberating empowerment of God's new reign. It is in, and through, the empowerment of the new companionship that Christ's 'divinity' is revealed. I recall a pertinent quotation attributed to the Canadian theologian, Gregory Baum: "God is what happens to a person on the way to becoming human." As those opposed to Jesus witnessed new breakthroughs supporting human advancement, they became more petrified, of both their own power, and what they perceived to be the divine validation and justification for exercising such power. Here we touch into a much deeper meaning of the miracle stories, not just as prodigious deeds but as creative parables at the service of empowering deliverance.

## *Discipleship of a Subversive King*

When people reclaim their voice, through the narrative of an empowering story, and when they learn to overcome the crippling paralysis of internalized oppression, they pose an enormous threat to every imperial system. Jesus was such a threat and the domination system did not tolerate him for long. Much more tragically is what Christendom did to the embryonic vision. The dream was firstly tamed, then domesticated, and finally institutionalized by Constantine's uncontrolled desire for absolute power.

When the doctrinal foundations were set in stone – firstly under the supervision of Constantine (Nicea) and later under Marcian (Chalcedon) - the primordial dream of the Companionship of Empowerment was seriously jeopardized. It was never totally suppressed, but was largely subverted for over 1500 years. Today it is poised to return with a vengeance, and the postcolonial impetus – among other contemporary movements – contributes significantly to this retrieval.

Jesus was eliminated – because of the dangerous empowerment he unleashed. And those whom the Gospels claim to have been his primary followers – the male apostles and disciples – were scattered. From earliest times, Christendom upheld the belief that the group known as the twelve (apostles) were quickly re-assembled, re-animated by the Holy Spirit, and resumed responsibility for the growth and development of what came to be known as the Church. As I indicate in the last Chapter, it is highly unlikely that the twelve returned (except possibly for Peter and James). Their acclaimed return in Acts (chapter 2) is a Lukan invention in order to lay solid apostolic foundations for his two patriarchal heroes, Peter and Paul. And in the process of inventing the male-based apostolic Church, Luke chose to subvert – possibly destroy - the original witnesses, namely the Gospel women who remained faithful through Calvary and Resurrection, and beyond into the opening decades of the infant Church.

Any postcolonial attempt at retrieving authentic Christian discipleship must face these sordid disturbing facts. The primary message of the Gospels, namely the Companionship of Empowerment, has been seriously undermined and domesticated to accommodate ecclesiastical power-mongering. Patriarchal heroic models dominate our perception and interpretation. We underrate the communal dimension, and the embedded nature of Gospel discipleship in the villages of rural Galilee, and the more egalitarian partnerships through which discipleship is mediated and culturally expressed.

## Sent Forth in Twos

Some postcolonial theorists make the argument that studying both dominant forms of knowledge and marginalized ones as binary opposites perpetuates their existence as homogeneous entities. Homi K. Bhabha feels the postcolonial world should valorize spaces of mixing; spaces where truth and authenticity move aside for ambiguity. This space of hybridity, he argues, offers the most profound challenge to colonialism. (Bhabha, 1994, 113). Initially, it seems that Jesus had quite a complex group of followers, already streamlined and stratified by the end of the first Christian century.

Christian discipleship tends to be perceived as an *individual* endeavor. Persons on their own are individually called to follow Christ more closely. This is evidenced in the miraculous call of St. Paul on the Damascus Road, and repeated many times in history in our portrayal of sainthood and holiness. In the Gospels, however, while the call is often portrayed in individual terms, the missioning is done in pairs (cf. Mk.6:7; Lk.10:1). And there is a strong emphasis on the domestic, non-patriarchal context, as disciples are sent, not to the imperial palace, nor to the temple, but to the villages, and the people's homes.

We need to confront this heroic myth and subject it to a postcolonial critique. In the Christian Gospels, we know of pairs of brothers (James and John) called to apostolic ministry. And it seems that husband-and-wife pairs also prevailed (Cleopas and his unnamed wife?). More controversial is the suggestion that sisters were also called, and this opens up new and disturbing insights on how Luke deals with the pair, Martha and Mary. *Diakonia* (serving) is the word used for *ministry* in Luke 10:40; it also occurs eight times in Acts. In every case, the word signifies acts of ministry in partnership with others, suggesting activity of mediation as a go-between. The work at hand encompasses acts of material relief and ministerial leadership as well as proclamation on behalf of the Christian community. Luke splits the two women into binary opposition, complimenting the passive one, and casting the active one in a negative light, an imposed interpretation that falsely designates both women.

Much more likely, Martha partnered Mary in co-leadership of a house church, caring for believers, preaching, and teaching. Martha and Mary as partners in ministry reflect important dimensions of *diakonia* (service) in Christian discipleship, particularly the essential relationship between hearing and doing the Word. Both Martha and Mary are called to hear and to do the Word, letting the Word sustain them in the process. According to Carter (1996), the learning of Mary and the doing of Martha belong together and should never be separated in dualistic splitting.

Gospel discipleship seems to have been more of a shared endeavor rather than an individual enterprise. And it modeled not the patriarchal hero of earlier times, but a new collaborative mutuality more congenial to the Companionship of Empowerment. It looks as if Paul wanted to honor that new collective mode of witness, drawing on the ecclesial secular groups as a basic model for the young evolving Church. Paul adopted a model used for local governance of towns and cities (*ecclesia*) but dramatically changed its ethos and modus operandi.

The early Pauline communities were small, fluid and flexible, mobilizing and celebrating the diverse gifts of the community for the common good of all. As reviewed above, Richard Horsley (1997; 2008) has consistently argued that Paul adopted an explicitly provocative anti-colonial stance, viewing these small communities as a counter-cultural force to Roman imperial domination. Just as the Empire set up regional structures to dominate and control, so the disciples of the Companionship of Empowerment organized small groups to empower the masses from the ground up. How extensive the groups became, and how consciously this anti-imperial vision was adopted, is difficult to retrieve with any degree of historical accuracy. It certainly did not survive Constantine's imperial onslaught.

Or did it? The history of the Christian Church proliferates with counter-cultural movements from the ground up. Perhaps, the most outstanding is that of the monastic and religious orders, whose finest witness has once more been tragically subverted. I refer particularly to the many women's movements which several Church history books don't even record, along with outstanding foundresses who provide us with far more daring prophetic action than many of the renowned male founders. This is material for another phase in postcolonial research, to expose and illuminate not merely the subverted power-games of the Scriptures, but the more intriguing and disturbing distortions that characterize the history of all the Christian Churches.

# Chapter 7:
# _Incarnating Subversive Wholeness_

_Memory is a powerful tool in resisting institutionally sanctioned forgetfulness._

Kwok Pui-Lan

_Like a sacred trickster, Jesus shows forth the shocking; performs perfidy; hails the hysterical; provides a hermeneutic for hyperbole; a syntax for sarcasm; and invents idioms of irony._

Marion Grau

Popular Christianity seeks to monopolize the theological notion of _Incarnation_. There is only one meaning that can be tolerated and entertained: _namely that about two thousand years ago, God sent Jesus to redeem sinful humanity._ And because the human body was perceived to be central to the corrupt human condition, then God had to come in a body like ours. It was a body like ours, yet significantly different in not being subject to the limitations of human nature, consistently described as 'sinfulness'. Because of this superior embodied condition, Jesus could bring about the 'redemption' of sin-prone humanity. And only the Christian Jesus is capable of doing that on behalf of all human creatures.

Thus the Christian Jesus becomes the only authentic Savior, not merely for Christians, but for all humans, including those who espouse other major religions. Indeed, there often prevails among Christians themselves a denominational fundamentalism whereby Catholics judge everybody else as not having access to the fullness of salvation, as do Southern Baptists in USA, and several other Christian groups around the world. Both within and beyond Christianity, Jesus has become an imperial Savior, the one and only expression of God's truth and deliverance for all humanity.

Let me draw the reader's attention to the heavy anthropocentric overlay in this ideology. Humans are deemed to be the cause of every flaw in the entire creation, planetary and cosmic alike. Creation is flawed, because humans have sinned. And by rectifying the human condition, it is assumed that creation can be brought back to a more wholesome state. Humans come first in every sense – everything else is usufruct for human use and well-being. Not merely is this a pernicious caricature of human nature (in its long evolutionary context), it also ensues in a deeply problematic understanding of what Christians call incarnation.

## A Flawed Anthropology

Firstly let us address the dysfunctional anthropology. Humans are portrayed as separated from and superior to everything else in creation. Humans are endowed with faculties which set them apart, more closely aligned with the governing God than any other creature in the universe. And only such human creatures can exert over the material creation the domination and control desired by God. God and humanity are aligned and congruent in a manner superior to all other life-forms.

This is the all-powerful God of patriarchal domination, the divine male king who rules from a 'perfect' realm beyond the earth. The perfection in question seems to be that of exercising infallible power. The right to colonize is unhindered, must not be obstructed, and every creature must submit unquestioningly to this 'divine' domination. According to the prevailing sanctioned myth, some angels did challenge this power, ensuing in a heavenly battle, in which the rebellious angels lost, were expelled from Heaven, landed on earth, and began to propagate the sinful human race.

Now God had lost the allegiance of his favored creatures, and yet God needed them to exert divine power over the vagrant creation. So the patriarchal God came up with a not very ingenious resolution. He sent his special Son (another patriarchal male) to become the ultimate scapegoat and victim, to pacify the anger of the great heavenly Lord, and thus win some semblance of restitution for sinful humanity. In theological terms, the plot came to be known as *atonement theory*. It deserves to be described as an ideology and not a theology.

The Christian religion is born out of this preposterous myth, variations of which can be detected in other major religions also. The Christian faith draws heavily on the formulations provided in classical Greek times. Thus Mark G. Brett (2008, 13) identifies a thread of continuity going from Aristotle to Augustine, to Thomas Aquinas:

> What is natural and just is that the soul rules over the body, that reason presides over the appetite. . . therefore, that wild beasts be subdued and subjected to the dominion of humanity. Therefore the man rules over the woman, the adult over the child, the father over his sons and daughters, that is to say the most powerful and perfect over those who are weakest and most imperfect.

Reflective religious adults of the 21st century totally reject myths of this nature. Nor does it seem possible – or worth the effort – to try and re-structure such myths. Adults suspect that such myths had spurious origins, and certainly in the twenty-first century, have outlived their usefulness.

One of the attractions of the postcolonial critique is that it creates openings to dream and recreate new myths, or revision old ones in a context relevant for the 21st. century. Essentially, postcolonialism exposes and illuminates the underlying dysfunctional power dynamics. In anthropological terms, it leads to the following critical questions:

- What does the story of humanity look like when we unmask the addiction to patriarchal power that has left us with an anthropology of crude reductionism and cultural shrinkage?

- As we strive to get beneath and behind the cult of patriarchal power, what alternative sources can furnish other insights into the meaning of human life?

- With a growing body of professional science tracing human history over several millions of years (see O'Murchu 2009), what alternative understandings of the human condition require our attention and discernment?

- Paleontology suggests that when humans remain very close to nature they tend to behave in more creative and responsible ways. Can we integrate this insight into those religious observations that consistently denounce the human as deviant, or do we need to get rid of such religiosity entirely?

- In one form or another all the religions propose a rescuing or redemption of flawed humanity. Is such a flawed condition an objective fact, or a concocted theory of patriarchal religion itself?

- Is the emphasis on human deviation not itself a ploy of patriarchal domination, to keep people subdued, inferior, guilty, thus making it easier for those in charge to exercise their insatiable desire for control and manipulation?

- And to what extent is the validation of such domination postulated on an imperial God-figure, himself a projection of the patriarchal will-to-power?

- Christians will question my disregard for revealed truth, and the canonicity of Sacred Scripture. Who drew up such ideas initially? Was it not a small elite male group of 3rd/4th centuries, with no regard for the wisdom of the rest of humanity, and half of God's creatures (namely the women) totally ignored? Critical reflective Christians of the 21st century find many of these doctrines archaic and irrelevant.

- And finally, is there a credible core in the Christian Gospels whereby we can piece together a more authentic, liberating and empowering way of being human? I believe there is, and it will be the basis of the reflections that constitute the remainder of this chapter.

## Towards a more Integrated Christian Anthropology

To begin with, we need to reclaim an understanding of the human congruent with our long historical and evolutionary unfolding. The proto-human is already evolving around 7,000,000 years ago, as evidenced by the discovery of the Toumai Skull in Chad (North Africa) in 2000 CE. And paleontologists who wish to remain within strictly-defined scientific boundaries, will readily concede that our walking-upright ancestors (Homo Erectus) who flourished in Africa some 3,000,000 years ago, were endowed with all the critical faculties that define the human as human.

That being the case, it seems to me a logical theological step to assert that God was fully at work – affirming unambiguously – in the evolution of the human throughout these past several thousand years. It beggars belief, therefore, that theologians are so reluctant to re-define what we mean by *Incarnation*. The incarnation of Holy Wisdom in the human did not begin with Jesus of Nazareth; it began in the savanna and woodlands of East Africa at least 3,000,000 years ago. Unfortunately, modern humans consistently fall foul of the patriarchal ploy to condemn everything that evolved prior to the patriarchal era itself, and thus project onto our ancient ancestors all the nasty stuff we don't like – much of which arises from the violent dysfunctionality of patriarchy itself.

In a previous work (O'Murchu 2009), I describe what an alternative Christian anthropology might look like, beginning with a relocating of divine human embodiment throughout our long evolutionary story of 7,000,000 years, thus transcending the narrow anthropocentric focus of the past 2,000 years. It seems to me that any reflective, spiritually-informed human person can discern sacred meaning in this story. Beginning with the assertion in the opening chapter of every catechism ever compiled, I believe that God has been fully at work in creation from the dawn of time. That same creative life-force has fully endorsed every significant breakthrough that characterizes the course of evolution, including that of the emergence of the human some 7,000, 000 years ago. Invoking the Pauline insight, the believer assumes, that when God says YES, God means precisely that (cf. 2Cor.1:18-20), an unambiguous affirmation of what emerges in every stage of creation's complex story.

If God is fully at work in our human emergence 7,000,000 years ago, and fully endorsing what is unfolding, then logically this is God's incarnational creativity flowering and flourishing in the human condition. This is where the incarnation of the human begins. From there on, God accompanies our human species ("I call you friends . . ." Jn.15:15) throughout the long complex journey of 7,000,000 years, a trajectory enjoying an ever greater scientific and cultural verification in contemporary scholarship (see Meredith 2011; Tattersall 2012).

The next logical question: Why then the historical Jesus? And to what purpose? Various scholars (Jaspers 1953; Armstrong 2006) suggest that the coming of Jesus happens in an axial era, a time of huge cultural upheaval and breakthrough, and in the midst of this time of transitional transformation God *affirms, confirms* and *celebrates* all that humanity had achieved over the 7,000,000 years. In and through the historical person of Jesus this affirmation and celebration is declared.

And we witness a parallel process in many (if not all) of the other great religions: The avatar of Hinduism, the bodhisatva of Buddhism, the prophet in Islam, the diviner in many indigenous African religions, the shaman in prehistoric times. God's incarnational affirmation of human unfolding is not merely a Christian revelation; it is a blessing shared with all human creatures irrespective of culture or religion. Restricting such liberation to the Christian context is another painful example of colonizing imperialism, which postcolonial wisdom seeks to expose and denounce.

The coming of God in Jesus has nothing to do with rescuing humanity from some ancient flaw of original sinfulness. Humans got it right most of the time – *precisely because we remained very close to nature.* And in so far as we got it wrong – and occasionally we made serious errors – Jesus modeled an adult way of being human whereby we are challenged to set things right for ourselves

147

rather than looking over our shoulder like dysfunctional children waiting for a patriarchal rescuer to sort things out on our behalf. John D. Crossan (2010, 89-90) suggests we should think in terms of God waiting on us, rather than we waiting on God, so that divine transformation on earth is facilitated through collaboration rather than by divine intervention. The challenge takes on added inspiration when expressed in poetry:

*Awaiting Collaboration, not Intervention*

*People were waiting, and still are, for intervention from on high.*
*A God who saves and rescues from a sphere beyond the sky.*
*The people wait anticipating,*
*And how long more will they be waiting*
*For a God of righteous judgment who already liberates.*

*Christian revelation happens within evolution's thrust*
*As humans reach a high point, the divine affirms first.*
*The focus on participating,*
*The challenge is for celebrating.*
*We wait for God to intervene, but God awaits on us.*

*Companions for Empowerment is the challenge of the hour,*
*An interactive process, a mission to empower.*
*The key word now: collaboration,*
*Undoing the power of domination,*
*Transgressing every boundary of patriarchal power.*

*The eschaton awaiting us is ours to co-create,*
*When justice, love, and truth engage, new hope to instigate.*
*The Gospels give the blueprint,*
*To guide us in discernment.*
*And dedicate ourselves afresh to our mission here on earth.*

It is this challenge to mature adulthood that is deeply inscribed in the Christian Gospels. It is also the dimension of our faith that has been most blatantly undermined throughout the 2000 years of Christendom.

## Incarnation within a Postcolonial Optic

Thus far I have been describing incarnation in exclusive human terms. And I have adopted the long evolutionary unfolding of our species, not merely the narrow context of the past 2,000 years. In a seminal work on incarnational theology, theologian, Sallie McFague (1993), provides an expanded horizon to understand afresh our meaning of the Christian notion of *Incarnation*. Instead of retaining focus on the historical person of Jesus, perceived to be superior to all other forms of God's presence in the world, we are invited to re-vision incarnation in terms of the created universe itself.

Embracing the oft-quoted words of Sallie McFague: God loves bodies, we postulate *embodiment* as the primary channel for incarnational endowment. It is in and through bodies that the creative imprint of God is most visibly etched throughout creation. Bodily existence is not merely a human prerogative. The universe itself is a body and so is planet Earth. All other creatures whether on earth or in the galactic realm are endowed with bodies, manifested on earth from the great primates to tiny bacteria. Embodiment seems to be the favoured divine medium through which truth and grace are revealed to humans.

When we humans annex something for our exclusive use, we are in danger of missing the convivial context of our existence, our relationship with Holy Mystery at the heart of creation. Every feature of our embodiment is inherited from the cosmic and planetary creation. Our bodily constitution, even our biological faculties, is gifted to us from the creative universe, through our grounded connectedness within the living earth itself (more in Shubin 2013). We are not sacred simply because we are endowed with souls. More accurately, the sacredness expressed through our soulfulness belongs to our groundedness in the physical creation itself (see Moore 1992).

Our human imperialism, often reinforced by our claim to be the creatures most closely related to God, undermines not merely the uniqueness of our humanity, but also that of our 'divinity'. By playing God, we succumb to an idolatry of our own making. We miss the context to which we long intimately, humanly and spiritually. We catapult ourselves into alienation and exile, blaming the sinfulness of a flawed creation, when in fact it is our dysfunctional relationship with that same creation that creates the alienation in the first place.

As earthlings, we are called to re-connect with the embodied realm cosmic and planetary life. This connection is upheld and reinforced in the missionary task of the Gospel itself. As indicated in a previous Chapter, Jesus sends the disciples into the *household*, represented by the home and the local village (bio-region). Moreover, Jesus often teaches in the open spaces and sends the disciples, not to the king's palace, nor to the temple, but into the local villages, to engage Gospel transformation in the convivial structure of household and local community. Poetry captivates the prophetic echoes of this transgressive move:

*From Empire to Household*

*Emmanuel among us has expanded sacred space*
*and redefines God's dwelling in our midst.*
*Beside the lake of Galilee the witnessing takes place,*
*while often on a mountain side, the preaching voice is raised;*
*the market-place and vineyard lead to parabolic trace.*

*It feels like God has broken out of sanctity's domain*
*while the sacred in our landscape we're unable to restrain.*

*The paradigm has shifted mid the echoes that endure*
*and centuries are needed to catch up.*
*From the Empire to the household is the lure*
*from the temple to the house-church we'll construe*
*and the fellowship at table we'll procure.*
*The greatest revolution proclaimed in sacred lore*
*with radical inclusiveness inscribed on every door.*

*Companions for empowerment command the way ahead*
*while the monarchy is largely lying in ruins.*
*The holy reign of kingship is shattered to the core,*
*the monarchy is scrambled and cannot long endure;*
*systematic patronizing no longer can procure.*
*An emerging dispensation setting every captive free,*
*subversively releasing prophetic liberty.*

*The kickback from the Empire requires a new response,*
*the power-games oft so slow to dissipate.*
*Like the monarch so intrusive mid the wedding feast,*
*disparaging inclusiveness, the core of Gospel yeast;*
*he must divide and conquer like every Empire's beast.*
*Companions for empowerment proactive must remain*
*till eventually the Empire collapses from the strain.*

*And the household symbolizing*
*the 'oikos' at the base,*
*becomes the new Jerusalem*
*Incarnation's sacred space.*

(*oikos* is the Greek word for house)

The cosmic and earthly creation forever seeks to enrich and empower us, as illustrated elegantly by the naturalist David Abram (2011). However, we are unable to receive and respond appropriately because we objectify and commodify the womb of our begetting, the well-spring of everything that endows our existence with grace and meaning. Our false sense of superiority, and our patriarchal manipulation of creation's resources, distorts and misrepresents the true meaning of our existence.

Incarnation, therefore, is not merely a divine endowment unique to humans. Incarnation is a process forever unfolding in our embodied evolution. It is an interactive process involving every form of embodied existence, including the paradoxical interweaving of death and new life. For Christians, Jesus is unique as an evolutionary prototype, providing an exemplary synthesis, of our past growth, our present engagement, and our future hope-filled becoming (cf. Ilio Delio 2008; 2011). By reducing Jesus to a Savior sent to rescue us from our flawed condition, we have grossly disfigured both the elegance of the human and the glory of God manifest in creation. We need a radical rediscovery of our faith as incarnational beings in God's embodied creation.

## Being Adult in our Faith

The Brazilian theologian, Ivone Gebara (2002, 7, 118) gets straight to the crux of Christianity's flawed anthropology in this perceptive statement:

> We need only to remember that in Christianity the aspect of sacrifice that is salvific is basically male. Male sacrifice is the only kind that redeems and restores life; male blood is the only blood of any value. . . . To cling to the Cross of Jesus as the major symbol of Christianity ultimately affirms the path of suffering and male martyrdom as the

only way to salvation and to highlight injustice towards women and humanity. All the suffering of women over the centuries of history would be deemed useless by such a theology of history.

The flawed anthropology is itself the progeny of a much more serious deviation, affecting women and men alike. The human has been extricated from its natural, God-given habitat. Born out of the womb of the earth, nourished and sustained by the fertile womb of the earth itself, the human is now so alienated from this planetary and cosmic origin that nothing short of a divine miracle is deemed adequate to rescue flawed humanity. In this colonized, co-dependent relationship, everything looks hopeless for the human, but when humans know no better, then the plight becomes normalized into theories of salvation and redemption which increasingly sound preposterous and incredible to adult faith-seekers of the 21$^{st}$ century.

The breakthrough for humanity will not be mediated by any imperial regime, divine or otherwise. As powerfully illustrated by naturalist, David Abram (2011), our redemption is postulated on a primeval return to the living earth itself, so that our carnal animality becomes the primary source of our empowerment, and not the cause of our damnation, which we have long been deluded to believe.

For too long we have colluded with a naïve faith of subjugation and passivity. We have behaved like obedient children to an imperial divine father-figure, indoctrinated into subordinated loyalty by unquestioningly accepting what we were told to believe. This is not merely a Christian strategy. It features in all the great religions, conditioned and transmitted so as to reinforce the patriarchal desire for absolute control. All the major religions use co-dependent language, inviting devotees to become children of a father-like God in a mother-like Church. The mutuality that befits adult exchange is notably absent.

Christians tend to project this childlike co-dependency back into the Gospels themselves. Jesus is portrayed as a loyal and obedient servant to a heavenly father, who demands even the untimely death of his beloved child. Jesus' command that we become like little children is liberally used in catechesis and prayer. The faithful disciple is the one who accepts unquestioningly what Jesus asks and demands. A kind of parental submission is admired and fostered.

Those who take to heart the Gospel call to seek first the Kingdom of God and its justice (cf. Matt. 6:33), grounded in the subversive empowerment of parable narratives, can scarcely avoid the conclusion that the wisdom of the Gospels targets not children and passive recipients, but adult people, called into fellowship with an adult Jesus, in the service of an adult God. *The adult is deeply inscribed into the vision of the Gospels,* focussed unambiguously on what I describe throughout this book as the Companionship of Empowerment.

## Empowering Women into Visibility

In the Christian Scriptures, both men and women succumb to co-dependent behavior, and both groups are consistently disempowered by the imperial forces of Roman and Jewish domination. From earliest times the Church has regarded the twelve apostles as the stalwarts of faith in God and in Jesus, but even a cursory reading of the Gospels highlights their fragility and vulnerability. The group known as the twelve seems somewhat stuck in the notion that Jesus should be some kind of imperial divine rescuer, and when he fails to live up to their expectations they all become quite petrified. As indicated later in this Chapter male identity as portrayed throughout the Gospels is fickle, unreliable, and deeply wounded.

Throughout the Gospels, as in the allied literature from the Roman and Greek worlds of the day, women tend to be described in terms of men, as spouse, parent or offspring. We have stories about Peter's mother-in-law, the daughter of Jairus, the Syrophoenician woman, the Samaritan woman, and in all cases the women have no names. The two people on the Emmaus road are assumed to be husband and wife; he is named (Cleopas), she remains unnamed.

Despite the fact that women in the Gospels seem to be relegated to inferior roles and cast within the prevailing patriarchal culture of submission and invisibility, most scholars go on to argue that Jesus adopted a very different stance, treating women with dignity and respect, including them in table fellowship, endorsing their participation in the Companionship of Empowerment. On a few occasions – the woman anointing his feet (Lk.7.36-50) and the Samaritan woman (Jn.4:4-42) – Jesus clearly transgresses the patriarchal and cultural expectations, with a damning verdict of the misogynist culture.

When it comes to the treatment of women in the Gospels, often Jesus seems to be playing an ambivalent – even a contradictory – role. A few scholars support the analysis of Kathleen Corley (2002), who exposes some serious flaws and limitations on how Jesus treats women. Even if we attribute these deviations to the Gospel writers (rather than to Jesus himself) we are still left with the personal and pastoral dilemma of sacred texts which are in conflict with the radical inclusiveness and empowerment of the new reign of God, the best known example being the story of the Syrphoenician woman (Mk.7:24-30).

Meanwhile, there is widespread agreement that both Jesus and Paul included women among their disciples. Much more controversial, but with growing evidence to support it, is the claim that some of those women played roles far more crucial than some of the twelve apostles. We have already encountered

Mary Magdalene, whose role as apostle to the apostles seems to be gaining acceptance and approval among a growing body of contemporary scholars (e.g., Brock 2003; King 2003; Bourgeault 2010). If this claim is eventually substantiated then indeed the Companionship of Empowerment will become a dangerous memory of enormous import.

All four Gospels highlight the presence of key women at the Cross and as the first witnesses to Resurrection breakthrough. In the various Gospels they are named as Mary Magdalene, Mary the mother of James, Salome, and Joanna. Mark (16:8) claims that they fled the scene of Calvary crippled with silent fear. How could Mark, whose portrayal of the male followers is so negative, allow himself to exonerate the women in the end? The men had fled, so in his misogynist fervour, Mark chooses to get rid of the women too.

## Women after the Resurrection

Postcolonial recapitulation won't allow Mark to get away with that. The other three Gospels, supported by apocryphal wisdom from early Christian times, not merely highlights the women's final fidelity to Jesus, but strongly hints at their proactive role in carrying forward the Christian message into the foundational communal experience upon which the Christian church is established. It was primarily the female disciples that kept alive the flame of faith in the weeks, months, and probably years after the events associated with the death and resurrection of Jesus. (More in Kim 2010, 118ff).

According to conventional Christian faith, all was confused and chaotic for a period of fifty days till the breakthrough came at Pentecost (Acts 2:1-11). Things got back on course with Peter championing the rise of the infant Church. A naïve literalism characterises this transition with no small measure of patriarchal manipulation. *Fifty* is a sacred number denoting a long period of time. It should never have been taken literally. The time-span in question is that of several months, possibly as long as ten years. *It was the women, and not the group of twelve, that laid the foundations of the infant church.* What precisely they did, and how they strategized their undertaking, we may never know, since –it seems – their achievements were never recorded. Worse still, their existence has scarcely been acknowledged.

The women named in the Pauline writings provide important clues to the central role played by these women as equals in ministry (cf. Borg & Crossan 2009, 50-53), and in some cases like that of Phoebe (Rm.16:1-2), with outstanding leadership abilities. Elizabeth Schussler Fiorenza (1983, 138-139) makes a brave attempt at retrieving what that early Christian female leadership would have looked like:

> Women were the first non-Jews to become members of the Jesus movement. . . .
> By keeping alive the good news of God's life-giving power in Jesus, the Galilean women continued the movement initiated by Jesus. Mary of Magdala was the most prominent of the Galilean disciples, because according to tradition she was the first one to receive a vision of the resurrected Lord. In the discipleship of equals, the role of women is not peripheral, but at the centre, and thus of utmost importance to the praxis of "solidarity from below."

Now comes the postcolonial critique: How do we rid Pentecost of its fixation on power and its repression of female discipleship? It was the women and not the men that got the Christian enterprise going, and sustained it for several years before male hegemony comes to the fore as depicted in the story of Acts. But is the story true? Did all the twelve come back after fleeing the Calvary scene? The only ones mentioned in either Acts or the Pauline literature are Peter and James; we never again here of the others. And if they did not return why did Luke create the scenario of Acts 2:1-11?

Did Luke feel he had to reconstruct an apostolic base – a kind of apostolic succession – to validate his two heroes, namely Peter and Paul? Peter emerges from the Pentecost experience as the heroic preacher, and his apostolic witness prepares the way for Luke's primary hero, namely Paul.

And why bring Mary, the mother of Jesus, into the scene? What is her symbolic significance? Is this Luke trying to resolve his guilty conscience? He has effectively obliterated the original disciples, namely, the women, and now tries to cover his back by substituting a token woman, albeit a highly significant one (the mother of Jesus), to compensate for those he has made insignificant – to the point of utter invisibility.

## Postcolonial Pneumatology

And the plot thickens further, when we apply the postcolonial critique to the text of Acts 2:1-11. It is noteworthy that we treat this text with a lopsided if not biased quality of interpretation. Think of the last time you heard a Pentecost homily on this passage – the chances are it focussed on the opening verses (1-4), with scant attention to the remaining section (5-11). We hail those empowered to teach and preach (the power basis), while ignoring those who *listen, hear, comprehend and discern* – all gifts of the Holy Spirit. How did this latter group acquire these gifts if –as the text indicates – they had not yet been evangelized?

Pneumatology faces a serious dilemma here – and also a formidable challenge. We recall the animating Spirit who hovered over the elemental creation (Gen.1:2), enlivening the original material, and inspiring everything in creation thereafter, including human beings. Is the latter group in Acts 2:5-11 not already exhibiting and bearing witness to the gifts of the Spirit at work in the whole of God's creation, humanity included? In which case, why doesn't the Pentecost homily focus on vv 5-11 instead of the exclusive attention often given to Acts 2:14? Presumably, because it does not suit the power politics being played out - then and now.

From a postcolonial perspective, Acts 2:1-4 carries a symbolic meaning, the nature of which has been grossly exaggerated. The text is better understood as that of a fresh injection of hope and meaning for the dejected group of 11/12 apostles, spiritually disheartened and disorientated after the untimely death of Jesus. They needed a fresh infusion of the Holy Spirit to get them back on track – bearing in mind that a mere few, and certainly not all, returned to the task of discipleship.

The full impact of Pentecost, however, is not in the first part (vv.1-4) but in the subsequent section (vv.5-11). This is the unimpeded Spirit blowing where she wills, awakening a discerning and faith-filled response, even among those who have not yet been evangelized. A timely and empowering reminder to all faith-seekers of the Great Spirit known to indigenous peoples – ancient and modern – for several millennia (more in O'Murchu 2012).

Belief in the Great Spirit is probably the oldest religion known to human beings, and probably also the most resilient and enduring. The Great Spirit is not a being as in the conventional Christian Trinity, but rather an embodied life-force percolating in every dimension of the created universe. It is the primary energizing source of everything in creation, divine and human alike. For first nations (indigenous) peoples, we encounter the Great Spirit primarily in the dynamic energetic flows of creation itself. These peoples do not worship the Great Spirit; instead they seek to co-create with it.

Is this the Spirit we encounter in Acts 2:5-11, in which an amorphous group of people, not yet evangelized (it seems), discern the unfolding wisdom amid the plethora of spoken languages? Were these peoples already filled with the living Spirit who brings to fruition everything in creation, and has been doing so long before the Lukan privileging of the twelve in the Upper room?

Far-fetched though some of these ideas might seem, a postcolonial critique requires us to examine afresh all texts – and contexts – that adopt power dynamics favouring the few and disempowering the many. Such disempowerment undermines any possibility of realizing authentic incarnational growth. And it certainly damages irreparably the liberating hope of that which constitutes the core of our Christian faith, namely the Companionship of Empowerment.

## Incarnational Masculinity

In the Gospels, we certainly need to revision and revamp the problematic use of gendered and genderizing distinctions. In many cases, women are treated with a repressed sense of anonymity, often made invisible and without the power of naming (as in the case of the first female disciples). Men, on the other hand, are cast as the powerful privileged ones, but when males fail to fulfil that culturally imposed role – and most actually fail to measure up - then the prevailing culture is merciless in relegating them – not merely into anonymity – but into crippling poverty, slavery, and the erosion of self-worth to the point of insanity.

The male subjects of several miracle stories, whether maimed, blind, dumb-and-deaf, or afflicted by evil spirits (read: internalized oppression), can scarcely be regarded as exemplary humans in any sense. They seem to be people of crushed spirit in broken bodies, culturally dislocated and socially disenfranchised. In such a culture, one wonders how many men came out winners in any significant sense? It sounds like a perpetually precarious plight in which the privileged few dominated from the top in some well-defined set of social or political roles, or one ran a high risk of being perpetually a non-person.

The Church has long regarded *the twelve apostles* as the stalwarts of faith in God and in Jesus, but even a cursory reading of the Gospels highlights their fragility and vulnerability. They seem somewhat stuck in the notion that Jesus should be some kind of imperial divine rescuer, and when he fails to live up to their expectations they consistently lose their bearings: Peter, forever needing reassurance to protect his power, and the brothers James and John preoccupied with their own privileged status in the life to come. Philip is quite unsure about future direction, while Thomas in the end wavers in doubt. And when it came to the final crunch, with Judas capitulating to total despair, the rest seem to flee, lest they too might suffer a similar plight. The malehood they exemplify is at best ambiguous, lacking many of the qualities which men of the time were expected to exhibit.

Coming to Jesus himself, Colleen M. Conway (2008), critically reviews how the male Jesus is portrayed throughout the New Testament, noting that the success of the empire centered around the notion of the emperor as the ideal man and the Roman citizen as one who aspired to be the same. Any person who was held up alongside the emperor as another source of authority would be assessed in terms of the cultural values represented in this Roman image of the 'manly man' or what Conway describes as 'hegemonic masculinity'. For both the apostles and the evangelists the image of Jesus tends to be that of the ideal Roman man, who occasionally breaks through the stereotype to reveal a quality of human vulnerability that would have been frowned upon at the time.

Conway's analysis is situated largely in a postcolonial context, illustrating how Jesus often ends up both mimicking yet contesting the hegemonic masculinity. She fails to mention other aspects of potential incarnational significance, e.g., Jesus's psychosexual identity. In a previous work, I outline the case for considering Jesus as an *androgyne* (O'Murchu 2011, 126ff). Transcending the dualistic split between male and female, Jesus, like other great prophetic figures, embodies a psychosexual identity with new potential for integration and human empowerment. Long maligned philosophically and socially, androgynous humanity is known to have flourished in several ancient cultures, and seems to be surfacing afresh in the fluid psycho-sexual identity that characterizes the 21$^{st}$. century. It carries liberating significance for males and females alike.

For both males and females, the Gospels fail to deliver a sense of incarnation come alive. The barrier seems to be mainly the disempowering impact of colonial power itself. What it inhibits more than anything else is the more collaborative, interdependent sense of human conviviality so central to the Companionship of Empowerment. Aristotelian autonomy and functionality haunt human personhood even within the Gospels themselves. Humans whose identity is molded around the web of living relationships – I call you friends and not servants – struggle to make a breakthrough in Gospel lore. They rarely succeed. That is an unfinished manifesto which adult Christians of the 21$^{st}$ century need to embrace afresh.

## Incarnation: an Expanded View

The functional anthropology of Aristotle and the imperial humanity of Constantine have jeopardized the evolutionary breakthrough of the Companionship of Empowerment. The human face of God made manifest in the community that centered around the historical Jesus has been scarred and desecrated, violated and distorted, by crude patriarchal reductionism. The fame of one-dimensional man existed long before Herbert Marcuse created the label. Incarnational humanity was subsumed into one narrow funnel with power, imperialism and patriarchy dictating all the key values.

Postcolonial wisdom requires us not merely to revisit the past distortions, but to offer alternative paradigms to make possible a more liberating and empowering future. In this process we must not abandon the past. The challenge facing us is to reclaim the past - that is, rework it - at greater depth beyond all the superficial accretions of more recent times. As a human species, our authentic God-directed story is not one of 2,000 years but a much more complex and elaborate epic of 7,000,000 years. This is where our theological reconstruction of Incarnation needs to start afresh.

Nor must we forget the earthy and cultural context of that evolutionary unfolding. For most of our time on earth, we humans got it right (or at least quite close to being right) because we remained very close to nature. In other words, we were embodied in the planetary web of life through which we reappropriated, time and again, a renewed embodied grounding in the cosmic creation itself. Throughout most of our evolutionary history, our incarnational embodiment has not been that of exclusive anthropocentrism, but that of a cosmic-planetary earthling, in and through which radiated the elegance of divine creativity.

When we re-center our Christian faith on the Companionship of Empowerment (Kingdom of God), then we glimpse in the life and ministry of the historical Jesus something of that expansive global sense of humanity. Jesus never identified with Aristotelian humanism, nor should the Church have sought to impose it upon him (in the councils of Nicea and Chalcedon). In the primordial vision of our Christian faith we evidence another way of being human, and being incarnational. Its reappropriation remains one of Christianity's most daunting challenges.

# Chapter 8:
# *Postcolonial Conversion for Colonial Christendom.*

*The historical Jesus would probably not recognize anything that they have done with him after his life, death and resurrection. As a humble craftsman, farmer, itinerant prophet, suffering servant, he would feel strange in the face of all the titles added to him, coming especially from the realm that he most criticized and condemned: that of power.*

Leonardo Boff

*The constant challenge a postcolonial critic faces is how to maintain marginal status. How to be on the edge. How to remain an outsider.*

R.S. Sugirtharajah

Postcolonial theology is about exploring "the manner in which faith and power relate in the postcolonial context." (Susan Abraham 2007, 45). More specifically, according to one of its best known advocates, R. S. Sugirtharajah (2012, 42), postcolonial biblical criticism engages with two challenges:
a) most of the biblical narratives come out of ancient colonial contexts and colonial tendencies were embedded in them; and
b) the Christian Bible and biblical interpretation played a pivotal role in maintaining a colonial religious culture right up to the present day.

Our task, therefore, as Christians informed by postcolonial insight, is to move into a more enlightened stance and engage more critically with the baggage we have naively assumed for far too long. A number of challenges spring to mind:

- cultivate a healthy suspicion about all inherited Christian wisdom;
- take nothing literally from the Scriptures;
- be vigilant around the power dynamics at work even in the sacred texts themselves;
- Look out for what was suppressed in order to uphold patriarchal power;
- Be wary of the patriarchal tendency to over-spiritualize, in order to subvert genuine adult seeking;
- Remember all history is about 'his-story'. How do we retrieve a more inclusive and justice-based understanding of history?
- How do we break the fetters of religious colonization, and undo the mental conditioning that still feeds so much religious ideology?

To address these challenges, I adopt the notion of *conversion*, despite the warning from R.S. Sugistharajah (2012, 181) that "Conversion with all its good intentions is essentially a colonizing act." Yet, the *metonoia* of the Christian Gospel is first and foremost a call to embrace the radical vision of the Companionship of Empowerment. It is not merely about turning away from a life of sin and futility, but forever striving to remain proactive in co-creating a world where justice and love can flourish.

The conversion envisaged in the present Chapter is much more than that of adopting an informed, critical and reflective stance around religious belief in general and around Christian faith in particular. It is a call to discern afresh how religion tends to appropriate the prevailing power-structures of a particular time and place, and use such power to colonize those it seeks to evangelize. The ensuing discernment – the envisaged conversion – is to expose the oppressive ingredients that camouflage as truth, to explore how we can dismantle their potential to indoctrinate, and how we can re-vision faith-commitment in terms of a more authentic original inspiration. These aspirations coalesce into the vision of the following poem:

*Metonoia on the Big Scale*

*The word metonia is subtle and free*
*And easily forged in false meaning.*
*It's not just reversing a sinful décor,*
*For a lifestyle of different leaning.*
*The word is nuanced towards larger embrace*
*With "noia" denoting the mind.*
*And "meta" translates not merely beyond,*
*But indicates largeness in kind.*

*A challenge arises both daunting and free,*
*Embrace a new mind to engage.*
*Break out of the confines imposed from of old,*
*Be wise like a seminal sage.*
*Examine convention and question its truth,*
*And query what dogma declares.*
*And opt for horizons that stretch and expand,*
*The Spirit embolden who dares.*

*I think, said Descartes, and therefore I am,*
*The rational ego's demur.*
*I am, says the sage, and therefore I think,*
*Is rich and profound in its lure.*

*The call to conversion, to mind and to heart:*
*Envision what's radically new.*
*And the cosmic expansion where God recreates*
*Is the home for all truth to pursue.*

In the case of Christianity, we will explore the conversion in terms of the following aspects of the inherited tradition:

1.  Christianity claims to be a monotheistic religion. What do we mean by monotheism? To what extent might it be another colonial veneer, used to reinforce not merely religious allegiance, but patriarchal domination as well?

2.  Christianity's long link with Judaism poses several challenges within a postcolonial critique. How do we convert to a deeper integration which many contemporary scripture scholars desire? And how do we change the violent God-images which recur so often in the Hebrew Scriptures?

3.  Is religious exclusivism meaningful in an age of global interdependence? Can we convert to an inclusive vision that celebrates commonalities rather than one that seeks to perpetuate and establish differences?

4.  How do we appropriate a relational anthropology, evolutionarily congruent, gender inclusive, and transcending the imperial clericalism that has reaped such havoc on Christian identity?

## Monotheism: Imperial Intent

In religious scholarship (especially in the West) the evolution of monotheism is widely considered to be a development of maturity

leading to deeper truth. Monotheism promotes the idea that God should be regarded as a unified wholeness. This can translate into an understanding of God as solely one – person or entity – as in the Muslim faith, or as a combination of descending expressions all accountable to one source (also called hethonism).
In the case of Christianity, despite its belief in three 'persons' named Father, Son, and Holy Spirit, there has always been a clear understanding that the diversity of the three is unambiguously subservient to the one overriding reality which Christians call *God*.

The rise of monotheistic religion is usually attributed to the Egyptian pharaoh, Akhenaton, in the fourteenth century BCE. Although the evidence is circumstantial, it seems that Moses, who lived around that time, assimilated this concept of one God, taking it into the desert with him. Thus the Jewish religion developed along monotheistic lines, and later, Christianity and Islam. However, Assmann (2010, 31) claims that the juxta-position of monotheism and polytheism arose from the theological debates of the seventeenth and eighteenth centuries. For some, the opposite of monotheism is not polytheism (worshipping many Gods), but the worship of false idols, thus failing to honor the one true God, the origin of unifying truth. The worship of false idols leads to false truths, while allegiance to the One God provides a more reliable pathway to unifying truth.

Jon Assmann suggests that the real opposite of monotheism is not polytheism but *cosmotheism*, the religion of an immanent God, which polytheistic belief systems strive to uphold by proposing various expressions of the divine in the divergent aspects of the created world. For Assmann therefore:

> The divine cannot be divorced from the world. Monotheism, however, sets out to do just that. The divine is emancipated from its symbiotic attachment to the

cosmos, society, and fate, and turns to face the world as a sovereign power. In the same stroke humanity is likewise emancipated form its symbiotic relationship with the world, and develops in partnership with the one God. (Assmann 2010, 41).

Thus the monotheistic deity reinforces the long history of patriarchal domination in a belief system that disempowers and disenfranchises not merely humans but the living earth itself, and the divine presence immanent in the whole creation. To this extent, monotheism resembles a political ideology rather than a religious belief

Laurel Schneider (2008) suggests that it is the impact of classical Greek philosophy that led to the evolution of monotheism as a dominant religious system. But where did the Greeks get the idea from? We cannot hope to answer this question with the rigorous detail scholars would wish to obtain. We can trace historical and cultural developments which support the desire for one unambiguous source for divine and earthly power. Echoes are discernible in the control and domination of the land - the shadow side of the agricultural revolution – some 10,000 years ago. The evolution of kingship some 5,000 years later is another significant landmark. The identification of God with earthly kingship can be detected in ancient Chinese and Indian religions going back to at least to 3,000 BCE. While the Greeks exerted strong literary and cultural influence on early Christianity, the more likely endorsement of monotheism comes from Jewish rather than Greek influence.

## Jewish Origins

When did Christianity become a religion in its own right? When – if ever – did it break away from its Jewish foundations and become a separate faith system? And more importantly, why? Many scripture scholars throughout the latter half of the 20th century argue for a closer liaison between the two faith systems. Scholars such as Geza Vermes, E.P. Sanders, Maurice Casey, Paula Fredriksen, Amy-Jill Levine all make a compelling case for the fact that Christianity is better understood as a revival or reform movement within Judaism. Judaism, therefore, is the true faith whereas Christianity is merely a kind of appendage to its growth and development.

William Arnal (2005) addresses several of the contentious issues related to the debate around the Jewish Jesus. Christianity's long endorsement of (or perhaps more accurately, collusion with) anti-Semitism is now universally condemned among Scripture scholars. There is also widespread recognition that we cannot hope to understand the New Testament in depth without a thorough knowledge of the Hebrew Scriptures. And nobody denies the Jewish inheritance of the historical Jesus, along with the formative influences that would have been part of his childhood and upbringing. Presuming, however, that Jesus remained loyal and faithful to all he imbibed from his Jewish culture, is based on assumptions that need a much more critical assessment.

Scripture scholars themselves can easily stand accused of a range of religious projections, related in several cases to their own faith base, and their formation as scholars in sacred learning, rendering them accountable to various denominations or institutions during their professional careers. Such a formative background can easily lend credence to the assumption (projection?) that Jesus was an eminently holy person who became deeply imbued in his native religion and remained loyal to its aspirations during his adult life. It is then a short step to envisage Jesus as a reformer of his own religion, seeking to establish it more authentically on the values of the Torah, as God's enduring law for right living.

One could argue of course that the deepest values embedded in the Jewish religion are precisely those envisioned in the Gospel project of the Kingdom of God (the new Companionship). In other words, the deepest values of Torah-based Judaism are similar to, if not identical with, those of authentic Christian faith. I suspect the American scholar, Thomas Sheehan (1986) would accept that conclusion, while ingeniously interpreting it very differently: *Jesus came to get rid of all formal religion, committing himself instead to a rediscovery of the sacred at the heart of God's creation.* And for Sheehan that rediscovery is eminently expressed in the Companionship of Empowerment.

If the pursuit of the Jewish Jesus ensues in some new kind of religious exclusivity, we are in danger of reinscribing the imperialism we need to get rid of. Instead let's use the purity of Torah-based faith, in conjunction with the deep values embedded in the new Companionship, to forge a novel spiritual alliance capable of celebrating not merely the best in both Judaism and Christianity, but indeed the unifying commonalities espoused by the deep story of all the great world religions.

## From Exclusive to Inclusive Belonging

In all the major religions known to humankind, exclusive loyalty commands the high ground. Hinduism has long prided itself in being a highly inclusive faith-system, yet in the closing decades of the 20th century Hindu fundamentalists carried out several barbaric attacks on Christian people and churches, particularly when the BJP party held political dominance. Overtly, Islam is probably the most forthright at the present time in asserting itself as the one true faith, in the face of which any infidel (which basically means every non-Muslim) runs the risk not merely of denunciation but of extermination. More subtly, several Christian sects and denominations also adhere to a self-righteous exclusivity: Jesus is declared to be unique among all the religions – which translates into Jesus being superior to all other religious figureheads.

For fundamentalist Christians, Jesus is the one and only way to salvation. And salvation or redemption is the primary, if not sole purpose of Christian faith. Even so-called progressive Christians concede that there is spiritual worth in other faith-systems, but not ultimate salvation. That alone belongs to the Christ of Christianity.

Imperialism still looms large in Christian teaching, preaching and cultural modeling. In February 2013, the Catholic Church elected a new Pope, after some days of deliberation, exclusively reserved to a group of senior Churchmen known as Cardinals, whose standard dress is modeled on royal imperial attire of early Roman times. These dominant males, most of whom were over 60 years of age, locked themselves into the inner chambers of the Vatican and in total secrecy from the world (and it seems from the rest of the Church) chose one of their members to be the next Pope.

All this was transpiring in the 21st-century world of mass information, a culture where access to information is deemed to be a central value to our more collaborative and egalitarian way of living, where open and transparent communication is considered an essential tool for effective community empowerment, where people feel valued when they are engaged more creatively in decision-making and discernment. In the election process of the new Pope we were witnessing an archaic patriarchal ritual, centered on power and domination. Moreover, it was all happening in Rome, the heart center of the Western imperial Church, at a time when 80% of Catholics live in the Southern hemisphere. It seems there is little room for a postcolonial critique, or a call to accountability, in such a solid bulwark of ecclesiastical domination.

Most disturbing of all was the media attention, voyeuristically following every development and highlighting every aspect of what some commentators rightly called a theatrical extravagance. Theatre can serve as a significant critique of what we so often take for granted. On this occasion, the commentaries seem to underplay the sense of exclusivity, and inadvertently ended up endorsing the colonial mimicry that is still so endemic to modern Catholicism – and to several other religious systems as well.

Very different is the missionary vision arising from the post-colonial reading rendered by Marion Grau (2011). Describing the initial ministry of Jesus as a *circumambulation*, a creative, boundary-transgressing walking around - culminating in the Companionship of Empowerment – Grau revisions contemporary Christian mission as a call ". . .to give voice to the ambivalent complexity and hybridity that mark peoples and lands without dissolving resolute senses of positionality and identity. . . .A circumambulation then, far from a victory march, articulates a lament of the way in which 'dangerous memories' are not allowed to haunt us, inform our communities, infect our perceptions of divinity, resurrect fears, whisper warnings, invoke translucent visions, invite unexpected and creative transformations of the Gospel." (Grau 2011, 3, 9).

The ambulating in question is slanted towards prophetic protest against all that oppresses and consigns to invisibility and elimination. More significantly, it embraces a new inclusivity – the preferential option for the poor and marginalized – laying the foundations for the Companionship of Empowerment. A new kind of freedom is released that moves the culture of faith towards greater diversity and multiplicity of expression. This is what modern commentators name as *multiple religious belonging*, described by Jose Maria Vigil (2010, 183, 186) in these words:

> There are many believers who have a plural religious experience, who live their religious experience in more than one religion. They have a double belonging or sometimes even a multiple belonging. . . . There is absolutely nothing exceptional in the experience of double or multiple religious belonging, even though that is still unimaginable for many of those who do not have the experience. . . .The possibility of an inter-religious theology already exists, even though it is in an experimental phase.[11]

This new sense of religious belonging transcends the denominational distinctions between churches and religions, including Judaism and Christianity. It involves a great deal more than mental assent to creeds or doctrines, to regular attendance at Church or Synagogue, or daily fidelity to religious prayer and devotion. It is a contemplative spirituality of deep seeing and bold liberating action. *Contemplation* and *Justice-making* become the complementary values to forge new empowering possibilities. *Contemplation* here signifies a mode of perception vividly described by Thomas Merton as the keen awareness of the interdependence of all things under God. This is the mystical gaze which liberation theologian, Leonardo Boff, depicts so insightfully:

> Mysticism is life itself apprehended in its radicalism and extreme density. Existence is endowed with gravity, buoyancy and depth when thus conceived and known appropriately. Mysticism always leads to the transcendence of all limits. It persuades us to examine other aspects of things than those we know, to suspect that reality is more than a mere structure concealing the realm of the absurd and the abyss, which can strike fear and anguish into our hearts. Mysticism teaches us instead that reality is where tenderness, receptivity and the mystery of loving kindness can

175

triumph and are encountered as joyful living, meaningful accomplishment, and a fruitful dream. . . . The mystic is not detached from history but committed to it as transformation, starting from a nucleus of transcendent meaning and a minimal utopian dimension which, in as much as it is religious, enables the mystic to be more perceptive than anyone else.

Leonardo Boff (1995, 161-162, 70).

The second dimension, that of *justice-making*, may be defined as the development of the vigorous relationships necessary to bring about the liberating empowerment of God's new reign on earth. It is a multi-disciplinary endeavor, breaking through all the dualistic splits that keep the secular and sacred apart. This integration requires a set of critical reflections, incorporating the following significant questions enumerated by Marion Grau (2011, 286):

- Who are the agents of inculturation?
- Who is left out, invisible, unrepresented?
- Who dominates, takes up more energy-time?
- What kinds of stereotypes and assumptions block the gentle spirit of careful transmutation and adaptation?

In this synthesis of contemplation and justice-making, we seek to outgrow the adversarial divisions that kept religions locked in often violent opposition, each seeking to outdo the others in the name of an ultimate patriarchal authority. Today, the authoritative, postcolonial truth is in the universal web of life, pre-existing all formal religion by millions of years. It is in the grounded coming together of all people of good-will whereby the shalom of Judaism, the peace of Christ, the Muslim salaam, and the ahimsa (non-violence) of Dharmic religion, all come to true fruition in

176

a shared spirituality stripped of the imperial violence that has dogged formal religion for far too long.

A key goal of post-colonial theorists is clearing space for multiple voices. This is especially true of those voices that have been previously silenced by dominant ideologies, described in postcolonial literature as the *subaltern*. As indicated in Chapter Two above, the notion of *hybridity* helps to describe the postcolonial conviction that new alliances embracing diversity and multiplicity should be seen as normative, and not merely marginal or exceptional. Bringing together the two concepts has several implications for both religion in general and for Christian faith particularly.

Today, mainline religion is critiqued from many different perspectives. The ambivalent attitude towards power, violence, and even warfare is frequently cited. As an embodiment of God's revelation for humanity, religion comes under severe strain. As Sugirtharajah (2012, 77) indicates, postcolonialism often views revelation as an ongoing process which embraces not only the Bible, tradition and the Church, but also other sacred texts and contemporary secular events. Today, revelation is often understood to belong primarily to creation at large, with each religion providing a particular historical and cultural articulation on how humans access and appropriate divine wisdom. In turn, this raises urgent questions of what it means to be human at this time, the subject to which we now turn our attention.

## Being Human in a new way

The human species still clings to the co-dependent mode of human relating, and the patronizing assimilation of other species. Many of our human institutions function on a pseudo-parental model, with those in charge perceived as parents and the rank-and-file treated as child-like dependents. Primary attention, culturally and organizationally, tends to be focused on those in charge: the prime minister, the CEO, the manager, the Bishop, the Imam, while a great deal of sensationalized news coverage is focused on those who deviate from, or rebel against, the co-dependent role. Those at the top are colonized by the patriarchal mind-set, and in turn colonize those over whom they exert control.

So long have we been doing it this way, it is difficult to envisage any alternative. We have sanctioned the process religiously (allegiance to the Sky God), and institutionalized it in a set of structures (social, political, economic, religious) that seem all but indispensible. Such is the hunger for unilateral power inherent to this way of operating, that we have subdued all other species, and the living earth itself, into useful commodities for imperial humanity. This extensive ecological exploitation, and its accompanying environmental degradation, progressively become humanity's greatest nightmare. Through the colonization of the natural world we are rapidly becoming the primary victims of our own destructive imperialism.

Since the mid-twentieth century, theorists of every persuasion have been advocating alternative models with the emphasis on *sustainability, conviviality,* and *collaboration.* A new vision on how to relate to one another and engage in a more organic way with the living Earth has evoked extensive attention and research. Cooperation and collaboration are not just attractive alternatives to the fierce competition and destructive violence that characterize the modern world. They are deemed to be more promising and empowering for all human engagement and for the exercise of our responsibilities as an Earth species. (more in de Waal 2010; Rifkin 2009). While the consciousness has shifted significantly – from the pyramid to the circle – the practice is lagging far behind.

We have an abundance of alternative economic systems (cf. Greco 2009; Eisenstein 2011), many tried and tested. Collaborative work practices are known to be not merely more empowering but financially more productive and fruitful (Gratton 2011). The Basic Ecclesial developments, in Central and South America in the 1970s and 1980s, awoke admiration and congruence in Christians all over the world. Socially and politically, NGO activity became a life-saver for several peoples in poorer nations. Social networking proliferated - and still does (see Hawken 2007).

The consciousness has changed and will continue to do so. Intuitively, the human species seems to realize that things could be different – and better. On the part of major institutions the resistance to change is fierce, and the threat of the evolving consciousness is even more scary. It appears that things will have to get much worse – economically and politically - before the alternative consciousness gains an upper hand. Colonial power never concedes – historically, it tends to be superseded by an alternative worldview. This is the notion of the paradigm shift, extensively documented by social analysts in the latter half of the 20th century.

The ensuing conversion is both personal and collective. A greater sense of individual awareness, resilience, and flexibility will be needed for the emerging future. It will be people en-dowed with such creative possibilities who are likely to pioneer the new collaborative ways of mutual enhancement. Vigilance around the destructive force of fierce competition (especially in education and social conditioning), and a resolute commitment to more organic collaborative ways of being and working, are the values needed to realize the potential of a postcolonial way of be-ing in the world.

## *Spirituality as Cultural Breakthrough*

The call to conversion centered around multi-faith dialogue is not merely one of being more favorably disposed to religions other than one's own, nor is it merely an endorsement of double or multiple religious belonging. It is a call to address the colonial posturing through which religions compete with each other, seeking to outwit one another in the name of an imperial God with a monolithic command of truth. In the name of this God people vie, compete, judge and condemn each other in an adversarial battle of wits, with distinctive violent underpinnings in the opening decades of the 21$^{st}$ century. The postcolonial conversion challenges us to search for commonalities rather than emphasizing differences, to transcend adversarial bickering with a concerted commitment to peace and justice-making, and above all, transcend the self-righteous imperialism that continues to feed violent religious ideologies in the modern world.

The prospect of the major religions leading to a new world alliance of dialogue and cooperation is eclipsed by the rise of *spirituality* in the closing decades of the 20$^{th}$ century. It is in this sphere – rather than among the religions – that we witness commonalities outstripping differences, a development often prematurely dismissed as a postmodern free-for-all. It may, in fact, be the crucial catalyst to bring about all the other transformative breakthroughs described in this book.

A vast literature now exists on this emerging spirituality (King 2009; Johnson & Ord 2012; Phipps 2012). It is quite a complex phenomenon, denoting a range of theories and practices, some of which are divergently contradictory. It has a distinctive evolutionary flavor – an evolutionary imperative of our time - which a number of theorists fail to acknowledge, and this seems important for a postcolonial evaluation.

The distinction between *spirituality* and *religion* is of crucial importance, one deemed to be suspect and superficial by those defending religion as the only authentic articulation of our relationship with the divine. Firstly, the emerging spiritual consciousness of our time considers religion too structured and institutional to embrace the evolving desire for spiritual connection and integration experienced today on an expanding global scale. Secondly, the dualistic split between sacred and secular, endemic to several major religions, is perceived to be false and destructive. Thirdly, the anthropocentric tenor of much formal religion, with primary (sometimes, exclusive) focus on human beings – and their salvation – is regarded as an injustice to the God whose revelation belongs to all creation. Lastly, the imperial power – and accompanying self-righteousness – perceived to be deeply embedded in formal religion, and its accompanying portrayal of God – is perceived to be based on a set of historically conditioned assumptions arising from human projections rather than originating in any divinely revealed source.[12]

The emerging spirituality carries a deep appeal in the modern world, although it frequently fails to translate into new generic possibilities for those who espouse it. Sometimes it can lead to even greater spiritual dislocation. It is very much an evolving reality, learning as we go along, experimenting with rite and ritual, and often bewildering for people seeking to integrate its wisdom with formal churches and religions. One of its most appealing features is the espousal of values seeking greater congruence with ecological, environmental and systemic justice, the new global ethic envisaged by Catholic theologian, Hans Kung in the 1990s (Hans Küng 1991; Kung & Kuschel 1993).

Seeking to make the world a better place, devoid of poverty, oppression, violence, and religious rivalries, is emerging as a primary goal, sometimes esoterically described as creating heaven on earth.

## Dismantling the Myth of Patriarchy.

As I conclude this book, I devote the final section to the issue underpinning all postcolonial reflection and analysis: *power*! As indicated previously, I trace the rise of patriarchal governance to the shadow side of the agricultural revolution – about 10,000 years ago. Its fundamental ideology can be summed up in the dynamic of *divide-and-conquer*. Weaken those who oppose you – using whatever strategy works to your advantage – by fragmenting their defenses. The primary institution reinforcing patriarchy is that of *kingship*, religiously validated in what came to be known as the divine right of kings. Inherently hierarchical in nature, those that occupy the higher layers of the pyramid are deemed to be closer to the ruling God, with those at the base perceived to be the sinful and unworthy. Its cultural endurance – over many millennia – can be attributed to its effective management of what is perceived to be a flawed problematic creation. Maintenance of law and order is assumed to be God's primary desire for the evolution and development of the created universe.

Power is exerted not merely through brutal force, as in warfare and violent conflict, but also through several subtle layers of indoctrination. Essentially, everybody must think like those at the top, for they alone are capable of interpreting the divine will and they alone have the right (and power) to reinforce it. Over time, religion became a primary instrument to reinforce the perceptual and cognitive indoctrination. Even in our contemporary world, when people go to the polls to vote for a new government, there is a subtle and powerful indoctrination at work. Having voted in one or more political parties to form a new government – on the basis of a set of promises made by contending parties – the people have little or no say on how the government performs for the next five/six years. Frequently, promises are broken, or substantially altered, but the voting public has no say in that matter. In many contemporary democratic governments, people exert and enjoy minimum – not maximum – power.

Throughout the contemporary world – in politics, economics, social policy, religion – the patriarchal will-to-power holds sway. This begets a collusive and co-dependent culture in which millions unreflectively go along with the system, and end up psychologically and socially disenfranchised. Any attempt at articulating an alternative approach will be subtly but effectively muted and disavowed. We see this subversion at work in the economic realm. For many years now, we have witnessed, on a global scale, the rise of several alternative economic strategies; a range of examples are cited by Greco (2009) and Eisenstein (2011). Many last for a number of years and clearly empower people in dynamic and creative ways. Critics are quick to suggest that capitalism endures because it knows a more-long term durability; they never point out that more empowering alternatives fail to flourish because of the corrosive monopoly of patriarchal culture.

In the face of patriarchy's unrelenting grip on power, the conversion required necessitates firstly *a subversive awareness that will not shy away from asking several penetrating questions*. Raising such questions contributes to the psychic awareness necessary for that threshold of consciousness required to bring about transformative change. Action follows thought – as we think, so we act. Without a distinctive shift in consciousness, the energy that maintained and sustains the many dysfunctional institutions of our time will remain entrenched – until it eventually spins itself out in evolutionary lethargy. Directly attacking the dysfunctional structures is not likely to be productive. *Shifting the underlying consciousness* is what will effectively rattle the idols.

Let's also keep a close eye on archetypal movements of our time, always invading our comfort zones with prophetic turbulence. Let me end with one such archetypal shaking-up of paradigms, a provocative story related to the first declaration of war on Iraq in 1991. Peace rallies were held in many big cities like London and New York. At one London rally, a group of the gay-and-lesbian people marched beneath a large banner which read: "*Take our men to bed, not to war.*" The provocative slogan caught the attention of world-wide media, appearing on a number of front-page tabloids the following day.

Undoubtedly, some saw it as a salacious reckless statement by people interested in propagating their own hedonistic agenda rather than securing world peace. On closer reflection, it might have been quite a prophetic declaration. The American philosopher, Sam Keen, writing in the 1980s, noted that the human species had made a significant shift in its articulation of archetypal values. These are the values that tend to be covert rather than overt, and often mark evolutionary transitions. One of the transitions noted by Keen was that of the shift from the *Hero* to the *Lover.* (Keen 1983; 1988).

The shift first became apparent in the USA when the soldiers came home from Vietnam and, contrary to former times, there was little adulation or celebration. They were not viewed or acclaimed as heroes; to the contrary many wondered why they went out in the first place. The American cultural consciousness was no longer intrigued by heroes, whereas several other controversial new age movements of the 1960s, transgressed and transcended boundaries related to intimate personal relationships. *In truth, it was in the bedroom, and not in the battlefield, that the new heroism was evolving.*

In this controversial naming, Sam Keen is describing what might well be a leading postcolonial breakthrough of our time, with enormous challenges for discernment and conversion. Across the humanly populated planet the institutions of marriage and traditional family life are under severe strain. These have been the long-cherished harbingers for patriarchal power and the culturally sanctioned values of domination and control.

Secondly, the private domain of sexual intimacy has outgrown its exclusive heterosexual couple configuration, safeguarding the male as the primary procreative force, and reserving human reproduction as a biological, male-dominated process. With the release of the new cultural metaphor of *the Lover*, the entire landscape of male-controlled intimacy has been significantly undermined, ensuing in widespread cultural disarray.

There then follows an invitation to conversion – cultural, social, religious – a process which has scarcely begun. All around us we witness a new sexual and relational fluidity which religions often condemn as reckless and promiscuous. The formal religious culture(s) fails to read the archetypal undercurrents. The secular culture is equally in the dark in terms of the deeper unfolding reality and, for the greater part, refuses to get too closely involved. In face of this cultural shift, most people live in denial, and therefore little is being done - in any sphere – to co-create the new psychosexual ethic so urgently needed today.

What we are actually witnessing is an evolutionary shift of seismic proportion, one where humans have little choice but to move with the unfolding process. To choose otherwise is a sure pathway to nihilism and death. Faced with such an evolutionary imperative we become its helpless victims or creative co-participants. Obviously, the latter is the only viable choice, and hopefully the reflections of this book will help, in however small a way, to co-create the consciousness necessary for the evolutionary leap forward. The ultimate goal is not a new justification for power, but a fresh release of an ancient human and spiritual archetype: the convivial empowerment of all living beings.

\*\*

Postcolonialism invites us to engage language and text with a critical mind and a discerning heart. The primary text

185

underpinning the reflections of this book is the New Testament, the foundational document that inspires and sustains Christian faith. Central to that document are the four Gospels, based initially on an oral tradition, transmitted through an ancient language(s) like Aramaic. We are told that the original hearers hung on to the words of Jesus, and so do we, despite the fact that the original vibrations have morphed several times into various translations, and have been embellished as expanded narratives. As people of faith, we still hang on to those words! Even in silence their wisdom endures, and in poetry, we can still recapture something of their subliminal inspiration:

*The People Hung on to his Words* (Lk.19:48)

*They sought to destroy him, he threatened their power,*
*His words and his actions the people devour.*
*While the system resources deplete,*
*and they struggle for daily needs meet,*
*they detect new empowerment released.*
*So they cling to his words as echoes endure*
*knowing deep in their hearts a hope that is true.*

*Words spoken wisely, subversively real,*
*The parable story no power can conceal.*
*The workers exploited too long,*
*a Samaritan can't get it wrong,*
*A woman with leaven's new song.*
*The tables are turned on the temple's regime*
*with chaos released for a dangerous dream.*

*His words are a treasure to hold in the heart,*
*empowering companions a breakthrough to start.*
*The freedom that all hearts desire*

186

*set free all the captives beyond the Empire*
*and liberate new life with hearts set on fire.*
*2000 years later, the people still cling*
*to empowering words and the hope that they bring.*

# ENDNOTES

1. The word applied to Julius Caesar as a deified person was "divus", not the distinct word "deus". Thus Augustus called himself "Divi filius", and not "Dei filius". The line between been god and god-like was at times less than clear to the population at large, and Augustus seems to have been aware of the necessity of keeping the ambiguity. However, the subtle semantic distinction was lost outside Rome, where Augustus began to be worshipped as a deity. The inscription, *Divi filius*, thus came to be used for Augustus, and while the precise meaning may have been ambiguous, few doubted his God-like status.

2. As a purely semantic mechanism, and to maintain ambiguity, the court of Augustus demanded that any worship given to an imperial figure was paid to the "position of emperor" rather than the person of the emperor. Later, Tiberius (emperor from 14–37 AD) came to be accepted as the son of *divus Augustus,* and Hadrian as the son of *divus Trajan.* By the end of the 1st century, the emperor Domitian was being called "dominus et deus" i.e. *master and god.*

3. Many Catholics have failed to see the significance of this anthropology in the development of Christian marriage, which was only declared a sacrament at the Council of Trent, with one clear raison d'etre: Christian marriage is for *the procreation of the species.* In other words, Christian marriage exists to serve biological reproduction with the male as the primary source of that propagation. It would be 400 years later, in 1962, before the Catholic

Church would redefine marriage giving priority to the communication of love and intimacy between the couple.

4. Co-dependency entered the social-work vocabulary mainly after 1980 to describe dysfunctional behavior in families where the abuse of alcohol was a serious problem. It also became popular among feminists to describe the subjugation and oppression that women often experienced in patriarchal structures. In the present work, it denotes the attitudes and behaviors whereby those in dominant positions expect everybody else to behave passively, like children should relate to parents in conventional family situations. In other words, co-dependency denotes the inability or unwillingness to engage the adult in the other.

5. Joerg Rieger (2007, 70ff) offers a fine overview of Constantine's influence on the emergence of Christianity particularly in the 4th and 5th centuries, noting that the Orthodox Church considers Constantine to be a saint, of equal importance to the Apostles. (Rieger, 72).

6. Most of the major religions describe revelation (what God has revealed) as truth above and beyond all others. The conventional colonial mind tends to be intolerant of diversity and multi-culturalism. It seeks to impose a sameness on all peoples, driven by a subconscious desire for absolute control over others and their destiny. Islamic nationalization strongly endorses this imposed sameness, despite the widespread emergence of new trans-national models of identity challenging what Paul Gilroy (1993) calls the certainty of *roots*, and the contingency of *routes*. The American theologian, Ilia Delio (2013) suggests that an evolutionary understanding of revelation is likely to be the most appropriate metanarrative for a future empowering sense of Christian faith.

7. Orville Boyd Jenkins is a self-described anthropological linguist, with an academic background in philosophy, sociology and theology, and many years of cultural research in Kenya, East Africa. Between 2002 and 2012, he has regularly updated his website: http://orvillejenkins.com/languages/aramaicprimacy.html in which he provides extensive information on various attempts at accessing ancient Aramaic renderings adopted by the historical Jesus, as well as the various efforts to understand ancient Aramaic through Hebrew, Greek and Syriac. He also provides extensive coverage on the popular translation known as the *Peshitta*.

8. I have listed aspects in the life and ministry of Jesus frequently cited as evidence for his departure from his indigenous Jewish religion. Scholars seeking to uphold the Jewish identity of Jesus, such as Maurice Casey, James Crossley, Amy Levine, and others, contest that the interpretation I offer is simplistic, and fails to honor the complexity and nuances of covenantal Judaism to which – they claim – Jesus adhered very closely. As I indicate elsewhere in this book, I accept and support the significance of Jesus' Jewish background. However, I am not convinced that Jesus himself closely adhered to his inherited religion as some scholars contend. And my reading of the New Testament evidence, following the line of most Scripture scholars, suggests to me that Jesus did depart significantly from his inherited faith – not out of any sense of rejection, but to highlight the trans-religious significance of his message for the renewal of all life, human and earthly alike.

9. In the Hebrew Scriptures notions of afterlife and resurrection are quite late developments. Restoring people to life occurs in various writings (e.g., 1 Kings 17:17-24; 2 Kings 4:32-37; 2 Kings 13:21) – not the same thing however, as the miraculous exaltation of someone considered to be a divine hero.

10. However, we cannot rule out a close intimate relationship with Mary Magdalene, the nature of which has been the subject of much voyeuristic speculation, highlighted in recent times by Dan Brown's controversial book, *The Da Vinci Code*. This may well be a matter for serious mystical discernment, as poignantly and sensitively illustrated by Cynthia Bourgeault in her highly original work on Mary Magdalene (Bourgeault 2010).

11. Multiple religious belonging is a very recent development which as yet has received scant scholarly attention. Johnson & Ord (2012) explore its meaning under the rubric of *interspirituality*, a concept initially coined by the late Wayne Teasdale (1945-2004), a Christian sanyasa (lay monk). Johnson & Ord offer two understandings: a) The coming together of world religions, with devotees embracing practices from the different religious systems in order to highlight commonalities rather than differences; advocates of formal religion tend to dismiss such endeavors as unhealthy forms of syncretism. b) The emerging significance in our time of spirituality, perceived to be superseding religion – Wayne Teasdale's interspirituality (Teasdale 1999). What unites the religions rather than what divides them is the primary concern, but spirituality also marks a new threshold whereby millions all over the world are attracted to religious values, transcendence, and mystical union without any grounding in formal religion.

12. Marion Grau (2011, 270) makes the further theological observation that: "The global resurgence of indigenous and pagan spiritualities may also have to do with the return of the repressed feminine divine that could not be accommodated in classical theism, focused on an all-male Trinity." Just one of several significant challenges to our inherited imperial theology.

# BIBLIOGRAPHY

Abram, David. 2011. *On Becoming Animal: An Earthly Cosmology,* New York: Random House.

Abraham, Susan. 2007. *Identity, Ethics and Non-Violence in Postcolonial Theory,* New York: Palgrave Macmillan

Armstrong, Karen. 2006. *The Great Transformation.* New York: Anchor Books.

Arnal, William. 2005. *The Symbolic Jesus.* Oakville, CT: Equinox.

Assmann, Jan. 2010. *The Price of Monotheism,* Stanford, CA: Stanford University Press.


Barker, Graeme. 2009. *The Agricultural Revolution in Prehistory.* Oxford (UK): Oxford University Press.

Bauckham, Richard. 2002. *Gospel Women.* Grand Rapids: Eerdmans.

Bhabha, Homi K. 1994. The Location of Culture. London: Routledge.

Boff, Leonardo. 1995. *Ecology and Liberation: A New Paradigm,* Maryknoll, NY: Orbis.
            2013. *Christianity in a Nutshell.* Maryknoll, NY: Orbis Books.

Borg, Marcus and John Dominic Crossan. 2009. *The First Paul,* New York: HarperCollins.

Bourgeault, Cynthia. 2008. *The Wisdom Jesus,* Boston: Shambala.
            2010. *The Meaning of Mary Magdalene,* Boston: Shambala.

Brett, Mark. 2008. *Decolonizing God: The Bible in the Tides of Empire.* Sheffield (UK): Phoenix Press.

Brock, Ann Graham. 2003. *Mary Magdalene, the First Apostle: The Struggle for Authority.* Cambridge, MA: Harvard University Press.

Brock, Rita N. & Rebecca Parker. 2008. *Saving Paradise.* Boston: Beacon Press.

Brueggemann, Walter. 1978. *The Prophetic Imagination.* Minn: Fortress Press.

1984. *The Hopeful Imagination.* Minn: Fortress Press.

Butler, Judith.1997. *The Psychic Life of Power: Theories in Subjection,* New York: Routledge.


Carter, Warren. 1996. "Getting Martha Out of the Kitchen : Luke 10:38-42," *Catholic Biblical Quarterly,* 58, 264-280

2001. *Matthew and Empire: Initial Explorations,* Harrisburg, PA: Trinity Press International.

2006. *The Roman Empire and the New Testament: An Essential Guide.* Nashville, TN: Abingdon Press.

Conway, Colleen M. 2008. *Behold the Man: Jesus and Greco-Roman Masculinity,* Oxford: Oxford University Press.

Cooper, Kate. 2013. *Band of Angels: The Forgotten World of Early Christian Women.* London (UK): Atlantic Books.

Corley, Kathleen. 2002. *Women and the Historical Jesus,* Santa Rosa, CA: Polebridge Press.

Craffert, Pieter. 2008. *The Life of a Galilean Shaman.* Eugene, OR: Cascade Books.

Crossan, John Dominic. 2007. *Christ and Empire.* San Francisco: Harper One.

2010. *The Greatest Prayer,* New York: HarperCollins.

2012. *The Power of Parable,* New York: HarperCollins.


David, J.R. 2013. *Internalized Oppression: The Psychology of Marginalized Groups.* New York: Springer.

Delio, Ilia. 2008. *Christ in Evolution*, Maryknoll, NY: Orbis Books.
2010. *The Emergent Christ*, Maryknoll, NY: Orbis Books.
2013. *The Unbearable Wholeness of Being*, Maryknoll, NY:
Orbis Books.
Dube, Muse W. 2000. *Postcolonial Feminist Interpretation of the Bible*,
Atlanta, GA: Chalice Press. 1998. "Saviour of the World but
not of this World," in R.S. Sugirtharajah, *The Postcolonial Bible*,
pp.118-135.
Dunn, James G.D. 1990. *Unity and Diversity in the New Testament*.
London: SCM Press.

Eisenstein, Charles. 2011. *Sacred Economics*. Berkeley, CA: Evolver
Editions.

Fanon, Frantz. 1963, *The Wretched of the Earth*. New York: Grove Press.

Gebara, Ivone. 2002. *Out of the Depths: Women's Experience of Evil
and Salvation*. Minn: Fortress Press.
Gilroy, Paul 1993. *The Black Atlantic: Modernity and Double-
Consciousness*, Cambridge, MA: Harvard University Press.
Gratton, Lynda. 2011. *The Shift: The Future of Work is Already Here*.
London: HarperCollins.
Grau, Marion. 2011. *Rethinking Mission in Postcolony*. New York:
Continuum/T.& T. Clark
Greco, Thomas. 2009. *The End of Money*, Edinburgh: Floris Books.

Hawken, Paul. 2007. *Blessed Unrest*. New York: Viking.
Hicks, John Mark. 1991. "The Parable of the Persistent Widow
(Luke 18:1-8)," *Restoration Quarterly* 33.4,
209-223.
Horsley, Richard. 1997. *Paul and Empire*, New York: Continuum.
1998. "Submerged Biblical Histories and
Imperial Biblical Studies," in Sugirtharajah,
*The Postcolonial Bible*, 152-173

2003. *Jesus and Empire: The Kingdom of God and the New World Disorder.* Minn: Fortress Press.
2008. *In the Shadow of Empire.* Louisville: Westminster John Knox Press.

Jaspers, Karl.1953. *The Origin and Goal of History.* London: Routledge and Kegan Paul.
Johnson, Kurt and David R. Ord. 2012. *The Coming Interspiritual Age.* Vancouver: Namaste Publishing.

Keen, Sam. 1983. *The Passionate Life.* London: Gateway Books.
1988. *Fire in the Belly.* New York: Bantam Books.
Kim, Seong Hee. 2010. *Mark, Women and Empire,* Sheffield (UK): Sheffield Phoenix Press.
Knight, Chris. 1991. Blood Relations: Menstruation and the Origins of Culture. New Haven: Yale University Press.
Korten, David. 2006. *From Empire to Earth Community,* San Francisco: Berrett-Koehler.
Kramer, Ross & Mary Rose d'Angelo. 1999. *Women and Christian Origins,* Oxford: Oxford University Press.
Kung, Hans. 1991. *Global Responsibility. In Search of a New World Ethic.* London: SCM Press.
Küng, Hans and Karl-Josef Kuschel (Eds.). 1993. *A Global Ethic. The Declaration of the Parliament of the World's Religions,* New York: Continuum.
Kurlansky, Mark. 2006. Nonviolence: Twenty-five Lessons from the History of a Dangerous Idea. New York: Jonathan Cape/ Random House.
Kwok, Pui-Lan. 2005. *Postcolonial Imagination and Feminist Theology.* Louisveille, KY: Westminster John Knox.

Licona, Michaelo R. 2010. *The Resurrection of Jesus: A New Historiographical Approach*, Downers Grove, IL: IVP Academic.
Liew, Tat-siong Benny. 1999a. *Politics of Parousia: Reading Mark Inter(con)textually, Leidin: Brill* 1999b. "Tyranny, Boundary and Might," *Journal for the Study of the New Testament.* 21, 7-31.
ED. 2009. *Postcolonial Interventions,* Sheffield (UK): Sheffield Phoenix Press.


Madigan, Kevin J. & Don J. Levinson. 2008. *Resurrection.* New Haven, CT: Yale University Press.
Marchal, Joseph. 2007. *The Politics of Heaven,* Minn: Fortress Press.
McFague, Sallie. 1993. *The Body of God: An Ecological Theology,* Minn: Fortress Press.
McLeod, John. 2010. *Beginning Postcolonialism,* Manchester:Manchester Univesity Press.
Mellody, Pia et al. 2003. *Facing Codependence.* New York: Harper & Row.
Meredith, Martin. 2011. *Born in Africa.* New York: Simon & Schuster.
Moore, Stephen D. (2006), *Empire and Apocalypse: Postcolonialism and the New Testament,* Sheffield: Sheffield Phoenix Press.
Moore, Thomas.1992. *Care of the Soul.* New York: Harper.
Morton, Stephen. 2007. *Gayatri Chakravorty Spivak.* New York: Routledge, 2007.
Moss, Candida. 2013. *The Myth of Persecution,* New York: Harper Collins.
Myers, Ched. 1988. *Binding the Strong Man,* Maryknoll, NY: Orbis Books.


Nolan, Albert. 1976 (2001). *Jesus before Christianity,* Maryknoll, NY: Orbis Books.

O'Grady, Selina. 2012. *And Man Created God: Kings, Cults and Conquerors at the time of Jesus.* London: Atlantic Books.

O'Murchu, Diarmuid 2009. *Ancestral Grace*, Maryknoll, NY: Orbis Books.

2010. *Adult Faith*, Maryknoll, NY: Orbis Books.

2012. *Christianity's Dangerous Memory.* New York: Crossroad.

2013. *The Meaning and Practice of Faith.* Maryknoll, NY: Orbis Books.

Peters, Ted et al. 2002. *Resurrection: Theological and Scientific Assessments.* Grand Rapids: Eerdmans.

Reid-Bowen, Paul. 2007. *Goddess as Nature*, Burlington, VT: Ashgate Books.

Rieger, Joerg. 2007. *Christ and Empire.* Minn: Fortress Press.

Runesson, Anna. 2011. *Exegesis in the Making: Postcolonialism and New Testament Studies*, Leidin (the Netherlands): Brill.

Rynne, Terrence J. 2008. *Gandhi and Jesus: The Saving Power of Non Violence*, Maryknoll, NY: *Orbis Books.*

Said, Edward. 1987. Orientalism. New York: Knopf/Doubleday.

1993. *Culture and Imperialism*, New York: Vintage.

Samuel, Simon. 2007. *A Postcolonial Reading of Mark's Story of Jesus*, New York: Continuum/T. & T. Clark.

Schneider, Laurel. 2008. *Beyond Monotheism: A Theology of Multiplicity*, New York: Routledge.

Schweitzer, Albert.1910. The Quest of the Historical Jesus; *A Critical Study Of Its Progress From Reimarus To Wrede*, London: A. & C. Black, (Augsburg Fortress Publishers, 2001 edition).

Schussler-Fiorenza, Elizabeth. 1983. *In Memory of Her.* London: SCM Press.

Segovia, Fernando. 1998. "Biblical Criticism and Postcolonial Studies: Toward a Postcolonial Optic," in Sugirtharajah, *The Postcolonial Bible.*, 49-65. 2009. "The Gospel of John," in Segovia & Sugirtharajah. *A Postcolonial Commentary . . .*, pp. 156-193.

Segovia, Fernando F. & R.S. Sugirtharajah EDS. 2009. *A Postcolonial Commentary on the New Testament Writings*, New York: Continuum/T. & T. Clark.

Sheehan, Thomas. 1986. *The First Coming.* New York: Random House.

Shubin, Neil. 2013. *The Universe Within: A Scientific Adventure.* New York: Allen Lane.

Sorokin, Pitrim. 1957. *Social and Cultural Dynamics: A Study of Change in Major Systems of Art, Truth, Ethics, Law and Social Relationships.* Boston, MA: *Porter Sargent Publishers.*

Stanley, Christopher. ED. 2011. *The Colonized Apostle: Paul through Postcolonial Eyes.* Minn: Fortress Press.

Sugirtharajah, R.S. 1998. *The Postcolonial Bible,* Sheffield: Sheffield Academic Press.
2002. *Postcolonial Criticism and Biblical Interpretation.* Oxford: Oxford University Press.
2005. *The Bible and Empire: Postcolonial Explorations.* Cambridge (UK): Cambridge University Press.
2012. *Exploring Postcolonial Biblical Criticism: History, Method, Practice.* New York: Wiley-Blackwell.

Tattersall, Ian. 2012. *Masters of the Planet.* New York: Palgrave Macmillan.

Taylor, Steve. 2005. *The Fall.* Winchester (UK): O Books.

Teasdale, Wayne. 1999. *The Mystic Heart: Discovering a Universal Spirituality in the World's Religions.* Novato, CA: New World Library.

Vigil, Jose Maria. 2010. *Toward a Planetary Theology*, Montreal: Dunamis Publishers.

Wilson, Schaef. 1986. *Co-Dependence: Misunderstood, Mistreated.* San Francisco: HarperSanFrancisco.
1988. *When Society Becomes an Addict.* San Francisco: Harper One.
Wright, Addison G. 1982. "The Widow's Mites: Praise or Lament," *Catholic Biblical Quarterly*, 44, 256-265.

Young, Robert J.C. 2003. *Postcolonialism.* Malden, MA: Blackwell.

33762214R00118

Made in the USA
Lexington, KY
11 July 2014